early

Visual
Skills

early

Visual Skills

Diana Williams

Please note that in this text 'she' is used to refer
to the child for the sake of clarity alone.

First published in 1998 by
Winslow Press Ltd, Telford Road, Bicester, Oxon OX6 0TS, United Kingdom
www.winslow-press.co.uk
Reprinted 2000

Copyright © Diana Williams, 1998

002–3736/Printed in the United Kingdom/**1030**

British Library Cataloguing in Publication Data
Williams, Diana, 1957 -
    Early Visual Skills
    1. Communicative disorders in children
    2. Developmentally disabled children
    I. Title
    371.9'14

ISBN 0 86388 187 4

EARLY VISUAL SKILLS
Contents

	Acknowledgements	vi
	Introduction	vii
SECTION 1	*Look & Learn*	1
SECTION 2	*Look at Me*	13
SECTION 3	*Let's Look Together*	25
SECTION 4	*Looking & Following*	35
SECTION 5	*Looking Around*	47
SECTION 6	*Visual Matching*	57
SECTION 7	*Visual Sorting*	83
SECTION 8	*Visual Sequencing*	109
SECTION 9	*Complex Visual Discrimination*	131
SECTION 10	*Visual Memory & Concentration*	163
SECTION 11	*Holiday Projects*	179
SECTION 12	*Visual Skills in the School Curriculum*	187
SECTION 13	*Visual Resources*	195
APPENDIX I	*Further Reading*	207
APPENDIX II	*Useful Addresses*	208

ACKNOWLEDGEMENTS

Thank you to all my friends and colleagues who have offered support and encouragement for this project. I would particulary like to thank Stephanie Martin for her advice and guidance. Once again I am also indebted to the children and families with whom I have worked and who have inspired the creation of this book.

INTRODUCTION

Early Visual Skills is intended for use by professionals who are working with children who have underdeveloped visual perceptual skills, associated with language delay or other communication difficulties. The activities are designed to stimulate and develop visual attention and discrimination skills.

Visual perceptual tasks are useful for developing specific concepts like colour, size and shape. They can also form part of an attention training programme. An additional benefit is that they provide the child with practice at hand–eye co-ordination.

The majority of the activities are non-verbal and are therefore suitable for children with limited spoken language. They are primarily aimed at the pre-school age group, but they can be modified to suit the needs of a range of children. For instance, older pupils at school can learn the associated vocabulary.

Professionals, parents and carers intending to use these activities should always consult appropriate specialists. The needs of the specific child should dictate who would be the best advisor. However, they would probably include some of the following: speech and language therapists, occupational therapists, teachers of the deaf or sensory impaired and teachers specializing in areas such as autism or learning difficulties. Children who present with speech, language or communication difficulties should be referred to a speech and language therapist.

HOW THE ACTIVITIES ARE ORGANIZED

Sections 1–10 of the manual cover visual attention, discrimination, sequencing, concentration and memory. Additional sections describe holiday listenings projects and topics for the school curriculum. A comprehensive list of materials and equipment is given at the end of the book.

The initial sections cover the basic visual experiences that are important to the development of the child's early communication skills. Later sections deal with more advanced perceptual skills, including visual matching, sorting and sequencing.

Each section describes teaching guidelines or activities designed to promote the development of the target visual skill. Activity sheets are provided with each teaching activity. They can be distributed to other professionals, parents or carers who may want to reinforce the child's learning. The activities on these sheets are aimed at helping the child to generalize the skills she has learnt in a structured setting to the home or school environment.

HOW TO USE THE ACTIVITIES

It is essential that activities are compatible with the child's visual and language abilities. The introduction to each section will help the user to decide whether the child is ready for a particular stage, or needs less advanced activities. Some visual skills, such as sequencing and memory activities, can be worked on simultaneously. Others follow a strict development sequence; for example, the child must be able to match colours before she can learn to sort them. The choice of activities will also depend on the individual child. For instance, a very withdrawn child may need to spend more time on developing eye-contact.

Teaching Activity

Sections 4–9 have several teaching activities. (Although these are for individual children, they can easily be adapted for groups.) These detailed activities will be particularly useful for students or professionals new to the area of language delay and visual perceptual skills. They can also be used as training material.

Useful Words and Phrases

A list of words and phrases has been included with each activity. This is intended only as a guideline, which the user may choose to omit. It is possible to demonstrate the expected responses to the child non-verbally in many of the activities. Alternatively, the user may decide to substitute other words and phrases which are more suited to the language and cultural needs of the individual child. The consistent use of instructions will provide structure to the activity and reinforce language development.

Increasing the Complexity of the Activity

Advice is provided on how the complexity of each teaching activity can be increased. These suggestions can be used to adapt the activity to the needs of the individual child.

Variations

A list of variations is included with each teaching activity. It has suggestions for similar activities and ideas on how to vary the teaching activity to satisfy the child's interests. These have a variety of developmental levels, so the adult needs to be aware of the child's overall capabilities when selecting alternative games. For example, an activity using picture material is developmentally more advanced for the child than one using large objects.

Activities Sheets for School or Nursery

Activities sheets for school or nursery accompany each teaching activity. The activities on these sheets are aimed at helping the child to generalize what she has learnt from structured activities to the school or nursery environment. They will also reinforce the child's learning of specific visual perceptual skills. The majority of the activities are for small groups or the whole class, with some suggestions for individual work.

One or more activities can be selected for the child. The following considerations should be borne in mind when selecting activities:

- the visual, cognitive, linguistic and developmental needs of the child;
- the child's everyday routines;
- the child's educational curriculum;
- the child's interests, likes and dislikes;
- the availability of materials;
- the teacher or nursery officer's preference for activities.

These considerations should be discussed with the education staff, and activities explained and demonstrated if possible.

The activities sheets for school or nursery can be photocopied and given to teachers and nursery staff. Tick the selected activities in the box provided. For example:

✔ Team-up by colour

In sports and games use colour to mark the different teams. The children select a sash from an assortment of colours. The children must get into groups according to the colour of their sashes.

Activities Sheets for Parents

Activities sheets for use at home accompany each teaching activity. They provide practical advice on using the child's everyday routines to stimulate visual awareness, and games to develop the child's visual perceptual skills.

The majority of the activities are for one-to-one work with a parent or other family member. There are some suggestions for group activities which could be played as a party game or with the child's friends.

One or more activities can be selected for the child. The following considerations should be borne in mind when selecting activities:

◆ the visual, cognitive, linguistic and developmental needs of the child;

◆ the child's everyday routines;

◆ the social and cultural context of the child;

◆ the child's interests, likes and dislikes;

◆ the availability of materials;

◆ the parent or carer's preference for activities.

These considerations should be discussed with the family, and activities explained and demonstrated if possible. The parent is not a teacher and therefore activities should avoid skills which are new or difficult for the child. The aim is for the family and child to enjoy the experience of learning together.

The activities sheets for parents can be photocopied and given to the child's family or carers. Tick the selected activities in the box provided. For example:

 Lap play

Sing and talk to your child while she is seated on your lap. You can kiss her, stroke her cheeks or pretend to nip her nose with your fingers.

List of Suitable Materials

A list of suitable materials, toys and other equipment is given for each target visual skill. These items have been selected as the most appropriate for the activities in a particular section. They include commercial products, standard educational equipment, everyday objects, toys, games and home-made items. The list can be photocopied and distributed to other professionals, parents and carers and should be used in conjunction with the corresponding activities sheet.

Advice should be given on the suitability of the equipment and materials for individual children. The child's cognitive, perceptual, linguistic and developmental level will determine the choice of materials. (See 'Toys and Materials for the Visually Impaired Child' and 'Choosing Materials for Teaching', below).

Professionals, parents or carers should be consulted regarding the child's preferences and the availability of items. After discussion, suitable items can be ticked. For example:

Look at Me: Alternative Materials and Equipment

A variety of items can be used for eye-contact games. For example:

Peek-a-boo games:

☐ scarf or piece of cloth   ☐ face mask

☐ shiny space blanket   ☐ book or magazine

☐ chiffon, net or lace   ☐ fan

Checklists

The checklists provide the parent or professional with a way of recording the child's activities and her response to these activities. Information should be recorded about the materials, type of activity, target visual skill and the response of the child. One example is provided for guidance at the top of each checklist.

SETTING UP LEARNING SITUATIONS

Follow these guidelines to make optimum use of the learning situation:

1 Check that the child is comfortable and ready to participate.

2 Make sure she is seated in a way that allows her maximum involvement in the activity. She should be able to see, touch and hear equipment and be able to move around easily if required.

3 Avoid visual distractions. Remember to:
- remove unwanted clutter from the table or floor space where you are working;
- avoid working near corridors, windows or any place where people may be walking past;
- keep away from busy wall displays and mirrors (if necessary, plain sheets of paper can be pinned over distracting material as a temporary measure);

◆ use a plain work surface (use a white piece of paper, cloth or board to cover patterned table cloths or carpets). If you have to work in a classroom or a nursery, try to have an uncluttered corner with plain walls that can be partitioned off. Use furniture such as a piano or a bookshelf to screen off the area. Other ideas include covering an old-fashioned clothes horse with a blanket or strategically placing a row of tall plants.

4 Reduce background noise. This is particularly important for children who have a sensory impairment and do not see or hear as well as they should.

5 Work in a well lit area, preferably with a source of natural light.

6 Carry out the activities with an adult who is known and liked by the child. She is more likely to co-operate and enjoy the games. A familiar person will also be able to observe and interpret the child's responses better.

7 Repeat the activities frequently. Constant repetition may be necessary to develop a child's skills.

For group activities:

1 Decide how you will seat the children. A circular or semi-circular arrangement is best, because it allows everybody a view of the material and the adult. Children with a sensory impairment may find it easier if they are seated in the middle of a semi-circle. This is the best position to hear and see the speaker.

2 Seat the children according to how well they work with other children and their own needs and preferences. An active child may attend better if she is seated between two quieter children. A passive child may sit still when at the outside of a semi-circle but needs adult help to make sure she participates.

PLANNING THE ACTIVITIES

1 Choose activities that are appropriate for the child's perceptual, cognitive, developmental and linguistic level.

2 Use the guidelines on increasing the complexity of the activity to expand her skills. The activities should build on the child's strengths and help to improve her visual perceptual skills.

3 Be clear about your aims for the activity: always check the child's record of progress to see if they are appropriate for her needs. (See 'Monitoring the Child's Progress', below.)

4 Decide which words or phrases are appropriate to use in the activity. (Select these from the list given for each activity, or substitute other words and phrases which are more suited to the language and cultural needs of the individual child.)

5 Decide on what responses you require from the child during the activity. This will depend on the type of activity, but also the abilities of the child. (See 'Responses from the Child', below.)

6 Plan the length of the activity. You need to allow enough time for the child to study materials visually. The length of the activity will also affect her concentration. (See Section 10 on *Concentration*.)

7 Use instructions that are clear, simple and within the language abilities of the child. The activities can be modified for children who have a limited understanding of spoken language. For example, the required responses can be modelled by the adult.

8 Decide which teaching strategies you will employ during the activity. Here are a few examples:

- ◆ *demonstration* — show the child the expected response to the activity, for example, replacing a shape in a puzzle;

- ◆ *providing a model* — give the child a model to copy, for example, a bridge made from bricks;

- ◆ *delayed imitation* — provide a model for the child, for example, a pattern of pegs, and then hide it out of sight. Can the child copy your model from memory? After completing the activity, the child can use your model to check her accuracy;

- ◆ *shadowing* — you have an identical set of equipment to that of the child, who is then able to copy each step of the task; for example, the child selects and threads a bead identical to yours;

◆ *backchaining* — the adult shows the child an activity and leaves her to carry out the last step, for example, adding the last bead to a sequence; the child is gradually expected to do more and more of the activity by herself;

◆ *frontchaining* — the child starts off an activity and the adult completes it; for example, the adult replaces the last few pieces in order to complete a puzzle. The child is gradually expected to do more and more of the activity by herself.

9 Plan how you will prompt the child if she needs help during the activity. Try the following cues:

◆ repetition of instructions;

◆ demonstration by the adult or another, more able, child of the expected reponse;

◆ pointing, physical manipulation or gesture;

◆ removing choices to increase the probability of the child making the correct response.

10 Part of the learning process involves reinforcing correct responses, so plan how you will praise the child and give feedback. Praise can be either verbal, as in "good girl", or non-verbal, like a hug or clap. Sometimes the repetition of the stimulus is a form of reward in itself: for example, repeating an action to make a puppet pop out. Always choose to give feedback in a form that the child is likely to understand.

If the child is to develop her visual skills, it is essential that she is also aware when she has made an incorrect response. Avoid being too negative. Help the child to respond correctly by using the prompts suggested above.

11 Adapt the activity to suit the individual child's level of concentration. (For more ideas on improving the child's concentration span, see Section 10 on *Concentration*.)

12 To maintain the child's interest, use the suggested variations and alternative equipment. Alternatively, ask the child to be the leader in the activities.

TOYS AND MATERIALS FOR THE VISUALLY IMPAIRED CHILD

Take extra care when selecting toys and materials for visually impaired children. The important factors are size, colour and contrast. Large, colourful toys are easier to see. The use of strong, primary colours and different textures can help emphasize either the overall shape or any small details. Multisensory toys provide extra interest for the child by combining movement, sound and touch with visual stimulation. Always check your choice of equipment with the child's therapist or teacher for sensory impairment.

Choosing materials for teaching

Activities may require the use of a variety of equipment, materials and toys. These need to be selected with care.

Remember:

1 A balance needs to be maintained between new and familiar equipment. Too many new things may frighten or bewilder a child, or overstimulate her so that she is unable to attend to the task; too many familiar items and she may become bored, making it difficult to maintain her interest.

2 Materials should be appropriate to the child's developmental, cognitive and linguistic level. The child's ability to recognize visual material follows a developmental sequence, so that object recognition will precede picture recognition. Use the following hierarchy when selecting materials:

- ☐ real objects
- ☐ large, doll-size toys
- ☐ miniature toys
- ☐ coloured photographs
- ☐ black and white photographs
- ☐ abstract line drawings

The amount of information shown in a picture is also important. Start with single-object pictures, and finally complex or composite pictures.

3 Toys and materials should be easy for the child to manipulate.

4 The child's interests, preferences and experiences should be taken into account when choosing materials.

5 Toys and materials that are interactive or provide the child with a challenge are more likely to hold her attention. Look for toys that stimulate visual exploration, demonstrate cause and effect, or involve problem solving.

6 Suitable materials are suggested at the beginning of each teaching activity. If these are not appropriate for the child, try the alternative materials listed for that teaching activity.

RESPONSES FROM THE CHILD

When planning activities you need to consider the responses the child is expected to make and how she will participate in the activity.

Remember:

1 A child may give a variety of responses to visual stimuli, including the following: looking at an object or event; following the eye-gaze or eye-point of another; a change in facial expression; making eye-contact; imitation of actions or events; reaching or pointing; talk, signs or gestures related to the stimuli.

2 Many of the activities require non-verbal responses so that even a child with limited spoken language can participate. Make it clear to the child how you expect her to participate in the activity by explaining or demonstrating the response.

3 Some responses are open to misinterpretation and you should look for patterns and consistencies before deciding whether a child's response can be judged as reliable.

   Be aware of responses that indicate the child is confused or misunderstanding and modify the activity accordingly.

4 The desired responses should be within the range of the child's overall capabilities, not just her visual perceptual skills: for example, if a child is expected to track a moving object visually, how good is her head control and balance? The other areas to consider are physical, auditory, cognitive, linguistic and social skills.

MONITORING THE CHILD'S PROGRESS

1 Record information about the activities you carry out with the child. It is useful to note the following information:

   ◆ *type of activity* — the area of visual skills being focused on, such as visual matching;

   ◆ *aims* — what you wanted to achieve with each child;

   ◆ *equipment* — materials and equipment used in the activity;

   ◆ *description of the activity* — name of the activity or a brief description;

   ◆ *teaching strategies* — describe the teaching strategies employed in presenting the activity;

   ◆ *organization of the activity* — individual or group session; any special arrangements should be noted;

   ◆ *expected response* — what you are expecting from the children.

For example:

Type of activity: visual sorting of colours. Colours to include red, blue, green and yellow.

Aims: to develop the ability to classify items according to their colour.

Equipment: four colour cards, and assorted objects in matching colours.

Description of the activity: 'My sorting box'.

Teaching strategies: demonstration of the task, using one object per colour card.

Organization of the activity: individual child working alone.

Expected response: to sort all objects within a 15-minute period.

2 Record what responses you expected the child to make and compare these with the child's actual responses in the activity. This information will help you decide if the activity is too easy or too difficult for the child.

Example of an individual record sheet:

Name of child	Andreas
Expected response	To build a tower of ten bricks
Actual response	Built a tower of five bricks, then knocked it down

Example of a group record sheet:

Expected response	Match big and small objects to a lotto board

Name of child	Response
Mira	Matching correctly
Kerry	Matching object but confusing size
Jafar	Matching some objects by size but not consistent

3 Make a note of the prompts and cues used by the adult to elicit the required response from the child. This information will also be useful in helping you to decide if the activity is too easy or too difficult for the child. The next stage may be to continue with the activity but gradually reduce the prompts and cues.

Example of an individual record sheet:

Name of child	Carlos
Expected response	To sort several items by colour without prompts
Actual responses	Sorted items after adult had demonstrated task three times

Example of a group record sheet:

Expected response	To sort several items by colour without prompts

Name	demonstration	repetition of instruction	pointing
Hang	/	/	/
Paul	/		
Teri	/	/	

SUMMARY OF ESSENTIAL POINTS

◆ Adapt activities to suit the child's visual needs.
◆ Select materials appropriate to the child's skills.
◆ Avoid visually distracting environments.
◆ Reduce background noise.
◆ Use appropriate language levels.
◆ Use familiar vocabulary.
◆ Look for consistent responses.
◆ Take into account the child's interests and preferences.
◆ Be aware of safety considerations.
◆ Record activities carefully.

HINTS FOR PARENTS

How to Help Your Child's Visual Skills

1 Use big and brightly coloured toys, as these will hold your child's attention longer.

2 Give her one toy or activity at a time.

3 Help you child to concentrate by clearing a space on the floor or a table. Cover patterned table cloths or carpets with a plain, white cloth, sheet or board.

4 Remember that your child may not get it right the first time. As long as your child is not bored, you can repeat activities as many times as you like.

5 You and your child will not be good playmates if either of you is hungry or sleepy. Choose a time that suits you as well as your child.

6 Activities should be fun for you and your child. If it seems like hard work, stop! You may need to try again at a different time or change the activity.

7 Do not worry if your child seems to lose interest quickly. Visually demanding tasks can be tiring for some children. Several short play sessions are better than one long one. Remember to vary the activities.

8 Help your child to concentrate by talking about and participating in the activity, rather than focusing on controlling her behaviour.

9 Stop the activity before she gets bored. This way she will be happy to return to the activity another time.

LOOK & LEARN

INTRODUCTION ◆ **3**

Teaching Guidelines 4
Activities for School or Nursery 5
Activities for Home 8
Alternative Materials & Equipment 11

LOOK & LEARN CHECKLIST ◆ **12**

SECTION 1

INTRODUCTION

A VARIED VISUAL experience is vital in building the young infant's understanding of objects and events in the world around her. This knowledge provides a foundation for the development of later cognition and language skills. Some children need support and guidance from the adult in attending to and making sense of what they see.

This section has ideas for encouraging the child to explore visually by herself. There are also suggestions for one-to-one games between adult and child, as well as group activities. Older children will find the activities a useful stimulus for expanding vocabulary, as part of topic-based work or for group discussions.

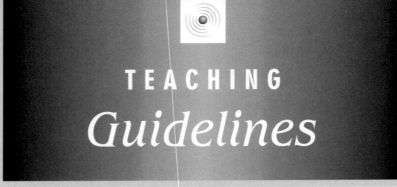

TEACHING
Guidelines

During the day, encourage the child to explore her environment visually. The following prompts will help her to attend and make sense of what she sees.

◆ *Use touch:* let the child feel what she is looking at; for example, trailing her fingers through water.

◆ *Encourage listening:* draw the child's attention to the sounds that accompany what she is seeing.

◆ *Make objects salient:* use various prompts to help the child notice different objects. You can show it to the child, point to it, say "look", use it to carry out an action, make it move, waving it about, for instance, or merely talk about it.

◆ *Provide variety:* vary the child's visual experience; for instance, seeing objects from different angles and in different positions.

◆ *Give the child time:* let her have a few minutes to study what she is looking at.

◆ *Repeat experiences:* repetition of experiences will help to consolidate the child's learning.

The position of the child is also important. Young children need to be seated upright in a comfortable position so they can view the events happening around them. For those children with limited mobility, care needs to be taken to ensure that things happen within their visual field.

Remember: objects and events should be visible to the child; toys that combine movement, sound and tactile experience will be of more interest to a visually impaired child.

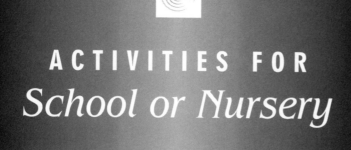

ACTIVITIES FOR
School or Nursery

During the day, provide a variety of visual experiences that allow the children to take an active role. Choose activities that emphasize shape, colour, size and texture. Here are a few suggestions.

☐ *Make a Look and Learn Corner*

Help the children collect objects and materials that are visually interesting. These could include:

☐ items made by the children

☐ pictures or photographs that represent a theme: for example, special events like weddings, seasonal snapshots, family members

☐ collections belonging to individual children: for example, football pictures

☐ pairs of items that share similar features, but which also have obvious differences: for example, a crayon and a piece of chalk, a bowl and a plate or a toothbrush and a hairbrush

☐ items that share an attribute: for example, a group of items that are all red or a set of miniatures

☐ pairs of items that are identical except for one attribute: for example, a square block and a rectangular block; a red glove and a blue glove

☐ objects and materials that represent a particular country or culture

☐ seasonal items: for example, sun glasses, suntan cream, holiday brochures

☐ fragile items (look but don't touch)

☐ items that you might put on your hands: for example, wedding rings, handcream, washing-up gloves, mittens or a finger bandage

- [ ] items that you might put on your feet: for example, shoes, socks, tights, sandals, flippers, wellington boots, slippers or corn plasters

- [ ] items that you might put on your head: for example, a baseball cap, glasses, wig, scarf, swimming hat, hair slide or headband

- [ ] objects from the past: for example, toys, household tools, clothes and books

- [ ] items associated with a particular place or occupation; so a ruler, eraser, pencil case, chalk and books might represent school, and a stethoscope, white coat, badge and medical book might represent a doctor

The look and learn corner will also offer a good resource for group discussion.

Make a collage

Collages are a great way of stimulating children to look. They are colourful and attractive, and involve only the simple skill of pasting. The best collages combine a variety of textures and shapes. Anything can be used, including household junk, scrap material and dried foods like pasta, grains and pulses. Try to think of a theme for your collage, such as different objects in the same colour, or the same objects in different colours. Enlist the help of the children in finding materials.

Explore painting

Painting is one way to encourage children to explore colour, shape and size. Pictures can be made using a variety of methods. Here are a few ideas:

- [ ] drop blobs of paint onto the paper, and blow them with a straw to make unusual patterns

- [ ] pipe cleaners can be put to a variety of uses: bend the ends to make different shapes like triangles or squares and use them to print patterns; dip one end in paint and drag it across the paper or make precise dots and dashes; dip the whole thing in paint and roll it across the paper

- [ ] try painting the edges of cotton reels, the wheels on toy cars or the edges of coins, then roll them across the paper

- [ ] use different materials to produce different effects; try sponge, rag, cotton wool, Plasticine and string, which can be dragged, dabbed or brushed across the paper

6

Early Visual Skills

□ show the children how to paint a butterfly. Fold a piece of paper in half, then open it out again. Paint half of the butterfly on one side of the paper, using large blobs of different coloured paint. Make sure that the paint comes up to the crease. Next fold the other half of the paper onto the painted side. Press down gently, so that the paint sticks to the clean side. Unfold the paper to reveal a beautiful butterfly (paint spread down the middle of the crease will look like a ghost or monster).

□ *Printing*

Make your own printing block by halving vegetables such as potatoes, swedes or turnips. Cut out various shapes from the flesh; these can be raised or hollow shapes. Other ideas are:

□ make prints using different body parts — try hands, fingertips, feet, toes, elbow, nose or knees

□ make 'lipstick prints' — make lots of different prints by changing lipstick colour and experimenting with different lip shapes

□ swap the traditional paint brush for a variety of everyday objects: use the edge of a ruler, the end of a cotton reel, shells, beads or dried pasta shapes to print different designs.

□ *Lucky dip box*

Make a lucky dip box. Ask at your local shop for an old display box used for crisps. These have a large hole at the front. Cover the box with shiny, colourful paper, and use strips of aluminium foil to form a curtain across the hole. Fill the box with items that are visually interesting: for example, a mirror, a hologram, a cartoon or photographs of the children. The children will have fun dipping their hand into the box and finding a toy. (See the 'Looking Box' in Section 13 for more ideas on items to put in the box.)

□ *Giant scrap box*

Make a giant scrap box using an empty cardboard box, (the bigger, the better). The children cover the box with pictures or cut-outs from magazines. Start with a few pictures and add to them each each day. The box will be a focal point of interest, stimulating talking as well as looking.

ACTIVITIES FOR
Home

Increase your child's awareness of the objects and events that surround her in her everyday life. She will be attracted by light, movement and colour. The act of looking can itself be made into a game. Here are some suggestions:

Looking at light

☐ torches that change colour

☐ a torch beam shone on a darkened wall

☐ pencil torches

☐ light reflecting on water (put a bowl of water on a sunny window sill)

☐ paper lanterns

☐ reflective paper

☐ Christmas fairy lights

☐ put a candle in a hollowed-out pumpkin at Halloween

☐ sunlight filtered through leaves

☐ contrast between light and shadow

☐ watch the sunrise or the sunset

☐ candles — birthday, coloured, floating or scented

! **Warning: Do not shine lights directly into the child's eyes. Flashing lights or similar equipment may trigger an epileptic or migraine attack in children prone to these conditions.**

Looking at water

- [ ] garden hoses or sprinklers
- [ ] fountains
- [ ] ponds, streams or rivers
- [ ] puddles
- [ ] fish tanks
- [ ] rain drops on the window
- [ ] dew on leaves, grass and flowers
- [ ] water in the washing up bowl
- [ ] fill plastic lemonade bottles with water. Watch how the water changes when you add paint, food colourings, bubble bath, tea, coffee or other drinking powders. Not all at the same time of course!
- [ ] splash in puddles, the bath or at the swimming pool
- [ ] experiment with sinking and floating — sail toy boats at the park; fill different containers at bath time and see how long they take to sink
- [ ] place some buoyant objects in an old plastic jar from the sweet shop. Half fill it with water. Seal the lid of the jar with glue or tape. The objects will bob about in the water as the jar is tipped from side to side.

Warning: Children are fascinated by water, so they do need careful supervision. Never leave a child alone with water.

Looking at pictures

- [ ] photo album
- [ ] scrapbook
- [ ] slide viewer
- [ ] picture cube
- [ ] advent calendars
- [ ] picture books
- [ ] flick book
- [ ] video films
- [ ] cinema
- [ ] birthday and other anniversary cards
- [ ] computer-generated images

Looking at movement

- [ ] dogs running in the park
- [ ] kites on a windy hilltop
- [ ] mobiles or chimes hung near a draughty window
- [ ] leaves blown by the wind
- [ ] washing flapping in a breeze
- [ ] fish swimming in an aquarium
- [ ] balloons tied to a buggy
- [ ] birds hopping in the garden
- [ ] falling snowflakes
- [ ] toys bobbing in the bath
- [ ] yo-yo

Looking through

- [ ] coloured cellophane
- [ ] a long tube (use the inside of a roll of wrapping paper)
- [ ] a short tube (use the inside of a toilet roll)
- [ ] holes cut in paper
- [ ] a magnifying glass
- [ ] a telescope
- [ ] binoculars
- [ ] a camera
- [ ] a kaleidoscope
- [ ] boxes with the ends removed
- [ ] toys with holes, such as large beads, construction pieces
- [ ] an octoscope

Looking at changes

- [ ] mixing an instant dessert mix
- [ ] adding food colouring to dough
- [ ] melting ice cubes
- [ ] making ice cubes or lollies
- [ ] mixing paints with water
- [ ] making bubbles with bubble bath
- [ ] watching flowers as they come into bloom
- [ ] growing cress or bulbs
- [ ] baking biscuits or cakes
- [ ] making popcorn or poppadoms
- [ ] watching snowflakes melting

Write down any other looking experiences your child has enjoyed.

ALTERNATIVE
Materials & Equipment

Section 13 lists a variety of toys, materials and equipment. These are listed according to their suitability for developing various visual skills. Look through educational catalogues, toy, gift, curio, joke, art and craft shops for more ideas.

Look & Learn
CHECKLIST

Child's name

Date	Activity	Comments
2.11	Looking at family album	Recognized mum, dad and sister

LOOK AT ME

INTRODUCTION ◆ **15**

Teaching Guidelines 16

Activities for School or Nursery 17

Activities for Home 19

Alternative Materials & Equipment 22

LOOK AT ME CHECKLIST ◆ **23**

SECTION 2

INTRODUCTION

THE ACTIVITIES in this section are designed to encourage the child to look at the adult. They aim to develop attention to the face and in particular to the eyes. The ability to give eye-contact is important in the development of a range of communication skills.

Looking at the face, like listening, is a way for the child to receive information. Additional cues from the speaker's facial expression, gestures and lip patterns will increase her understanding of speech and language. It is also a means by which the child can receive feedback about the effect of her actions and speech on others. For children with a hearing loss, this second channel is critical.

Eye-contact is also an important social skill. We look at people to show that we are interested and paying attention. In conversation, eye-contact is used to regulate turn taking between speakers. It acts as a signal to indicate who talks and when they talk.

Children who are developmentally delayed or have difficulties with social interaction often need specific help in initiating and sustaining eye-contact. This section offers suggestions for toys and games to encourage these children to develop this skill. The nature of the skill demands that the activities be carried out on a one-to-one basis. Guidelines are provided on ways to set up these individual sessions.

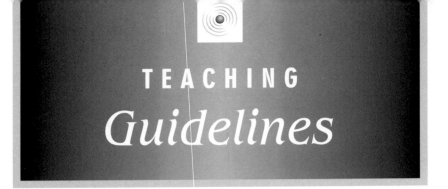

TEACHING
Guidelines

Use the following guidelines when planning a session with the child:

◆ Position yourself so that the child can easily see your face, even if this means lying down on the floor.

◆ Establish a rapport with the child first by engaging her attention and talking to her. Allow the child a few minutes to warm up before you start the games.

◆ Never force a child to look at you. Some children may find eye-contact with another person strange and frightening.

◆ Be aware of difficulties the child may have with head control. Seek the advice of a physiotherapist on supporting the child's posture. Remember you can always change your position.

◆ Let the child have times when she can look away. Staring is as socially unacceptable as avoiding eye-contact.

◆ Remember to make your facial expression interesting.

◆ A lively intonation and a higher pitched voice will also help to attract the child's attention.

ACTIVITIES FOR
School or Nursery

All activities for encouraging eye-contact have one thing in common: making the eyes and face interesting enough to attract the attention of the child. Here are some suggestions:

☐ *Face masks*

Make or buy some face masks. Put one on and then surprise the child with a loud "boo!" as you drop the mask from your face. Let the child have a turn. Masks with holes for the eyes and mouth allow you to attract the child's attention by batting your eyelashes or sticking your tongue out and wiggling it.

☐ *Peek-a-boo eyes*

Use eye masks designed for masquerades or fancy dress. These usually have a stick handle that allows you to hold the mask in front of your eyes. The mask can be quickly lowered, raised or moved to the side.

Alternatively, cover your eyes with two silver or gold foil cases used for cup cakes or jam tarts.

☐ *Face painting*

Try face painting, but paint your face as well as the child's!

☐ *Naughty puppet*

Play silly games with the naughty puppet who dances on your head, hides behind your back and sits on your shoulder.

Pop the puppet

Children love to see the puppet pop out. Move the toy where the child can see it and then pop out the puppet. Hide him again and this time move the toy nearer to your face.

Wigs

The luminous colours and shimmery quality of fun wigs are very attractive to children. Put them on your head back to front, then peek out from between the strands. Encourage the child to look for your hidden face.

Finger games

Make the shape of a butterfly or a bird with your hands. Let it flutter around your face. Try other shapes. Two hands opening and closing look like the mouth of a giant crocodile. You can build up the suspense by pretending you are going to bite the child's chin or nose. Shapes that represent a duck or a bird can be accompanied by quacking or chirping sounds. (Remember to keep your hands close to your face.)

Can you see me?

Use large floppy hats that fall down over your head. Encourage the child to lift the hat to find your face. If the child finds this difficult, start by covering your face with some see-through material such as net curtain, lace or chiffon. This way your face is only partially hidden.

I can see you

Look through a large tube at the child. Does she look back at you? Try using two old toilet rolls to make some binoculars, or a tube from a sheet of wrapping paper to make a telescope.

Listen and look

Use a squeaky toy to attract the child's attention. Hold it close to your face. If the child looks away, stop making the sound. (Swap the squeaky toy for other noise makers, such as rattles, party blowers, bells, hooters, shakers and whistles.)

'Look at me' eyes

Make your eyes interesting to look at. Use fun glasses, false eyelashes, or glittery make-up around your eyes.

ACTIVITIES FOR
Home

The following games are designed to encourage your child to look at your face and eyes. These simple games can be easily incorporated into the child's daily routine.

☐ *Peek-a-boo*

Your child will love 'peek-a-boo'. It is a great way of encouraging her to look at your face, and you can play it at any time or in any place. The basic game is to cover your face with your hands for a few seconds, asking "Where's mummy/grandpa/Susan?", then peeking out between them, calling "boo!". Your intonation and facial expression are all part of the game. They should surprise your child, but not frighten her.

You can also try hiding your face behind a book, peeking out from behind the curtains or popping up from behind the sofa. Encourage your child to be the active partner in the game. Take advantage of everyday situations where her face is momentarily hidden: for example, when dressing her, say "boo!" as she pushes her head through the neck of her jumper.

☐ *Songs and rhymes*

Songs and rhymes that have actions involving the hands and face will encourage your child to look at you. Try *Pat-a-Cake, Two Little Dickie-Birds, This is the way we wash our face; this is the way we comb our hair* or *Shoulders, head, knees and toes.*

Songs and rhymes that use sounds to build up anticipation will also encourage your child to look at your face. For example, the sneeze in *Ring-a-ring of Roses* can be drawn out to increase the tension: aaaah — tisshoo!

Lap play

Sing and talk to your child while she is seated on your lap. You can kiss her, stroke her cheeks or pretend to nip her nose with your fingers.

Everyday routines

Remember to include your child in your everyday routines. Activities like mummy putting on her make-up, auntie combing her hair or daddy shaving will arouse the interest of your child.

Fan

Attract your child's attention by fluttering a fan around your face. Hide behind it, then peep out from above or to the side of it.

Funny faces

Make your child laugh at your funny faces. Change your expression from a smile to a look of surprise. Or concentrate on moving one part of the face, for example raising your eyebrows or sticking your tongue out and giving it a wiggle. If you are really clever you can wiggle your ears!

Make different noises and sounds to add interest. Try ones that have very different lip shapes. For example, your lips are pushed out for 'sh', rounded for 'oo' and spread for 'ee'.

Nodding dog

Try making lots of movements with your head like the nodding dogs that are placed in the back window of cars. You can sway from side to side, nod up and down, or gently move it in a circle. Unlike the nodding dog, you can also zoom in close to your child's face, then pull away.

Wear something on your head that will move with you: for example, a head band with feathers, a hat with a pompom or a hair tie with long strings of beads. Try putting a bean bag on your head. Your child will have fun seeing how long it takes before it falls off. (This game can be combined with the 'Funny faces' game above.)

Dressing up

Play a dressing up game with scarves, hats and funny glasses. You can use the items around the rest of the body as well as the head. Try wrapping the scarf round your waist, prop the glasses on your head, or stick a hat on your foot.

☐ *Mirror play*

This adds variety to the above games. Both you and your child can sit looking into a large mirror. She will be fascinated by both her own reflection and yours.

☐ *Play time*

Remember there are often moments during play when eye-contact between you and your child is a natural occurrence: for instance, occasions like pushing her on a swing (from in front) or catching her as she comes down a slide. If she seems uninterested, try 'Nodding dogs' and 'Funny faces' to attract her attention.

☐ *Rough and tumble games*

Games involving physical play provide many opportunities to encourage eye-contact. You can lift your child up in the air so that she is looking down at you; bounce her on your knee, then pretend to drop her between your legs; or rock gently backwards and forwards with her facing you in your arms. These games can be combined with songs, like *This is the way the farmer rides* and *Ride a Cock-horse*.

ALTERNATIVE
Materials & Equipment

A variety of items can be used for eye-contact games. For example:

Peek-a-boo games

- [ ] scarf or piece of cloth
- [ ] shiny space blanket
- [ ] chiffon, net or lace
- [ ] face mask
- [ ] book or magazine
- [ ] fan

Focus on the eyes

- [ ] sunglasses or a fun pair of glasses
- [ ] cardboard tubes from inside the rolls of wrapping paper
- [ ] old toilet rolls
- [ ] glittery face and body paints
- [ ] fancy dress or masquerade eye masks
- [ ] silver and gold foil cake cases
- [ ] false eyelashes

Focus on the face and head

- [ ] face paints
- [ ] false moustache
- [ ] floppy hat or a hat with pompoms
- [ ] fun wigs
- [ ] glove, finger and pop-up puppets
- [ ] fan
- [ ] squeaky toys
- [ ] rattle, bell or shaker
- [ ] party blower
- [ ] hooter
- [ ] head band with feathers
- [ ] bean bag
- [ ] hair tie with beads

Look at Me
CHECKLIST

Child's name

Date	Activity	Comments
14/6	Peek–a–boo	Looking in anticipation. Copied "boo"

LET'S LOOK TOGETHER

INTRODUCTION ◆ 27

Teaching Guidelines 28

Activities for School or Nursery 29

Activities for Home 31

Alternative Materials & Equipment 33

LET'S LOOK TOGETHER CHECKLIST ◆ 34

S E C T I O N

3

INTRODUCTION

THIS SECTION contains activities where the adult and the child focus their attention on the same object or event. Mutual play of this sort helps attention, turn taking, concentration and language development. The child learns to attend to both an object and a person. In addition, conversations related to shared experiences of this sort are naturally more meaningful for the child.

Some activities are non-verbal, and would particularly benefit those children who have difficulty in listening to the adult while engaging in play. Other more complex activities involving spoken language provide a useful focus for joint conversation between the adult and the child.

TEACHING
Guidelines

Use the following guidelines to help you plan activities for sharing attention.

Observe the child to find out what objects or events have attracted her attention. Focus on these for your shared play activities.

Some children may need the adult to introduce appropriate toys and activities. Choose toys that allow the child to be an active partner: for example, action toys that move or make a noise at the press of a button or a lever.

Encourage the child's interest in the toy by looking, listening and playing with it yourself. Talk about it. Show the child how it works and what can be done with it.

Focus your talk on the activity. Comment on what you can see, the actions of the child, and what you or the child are about to do. But remember to allow the child quiet times to concentrate on looking.

Some children may find it difficult to share their play with an adult directly. Start by playing alongside the child with a duplicate set of toys. At first she may just copy your play. Gradually work towards becoming involved in her play. For instance, you can give her a piece to fit in her puzzle, or place a brick on top of her tower.

Joint attention can be achieved in a variety of ways. Here are some ideas:

- taking turns with the child by carrying out a similar action, such as both rolling a ball backwards and forwards;

- taking turns with the child, but taking a different role, such as kicking a ball for the child to catch;

- facilitating the child's play, for example keeping a stack of beakers steady while the child completes building a tower;

- extending the child's play, for example showing the child how a tambourine can be tapped as well as shaken;

- sharing experiences: for example, you and the child take turns in looking through a kaleidoscope.

ACTIVITIES FOR
School or Nursery

These activities provide the opportunity for the child and adult to look at toys and games together. Sharing attention is an important stage in developing turn-taking skills. These activities will also serve as a focus for conversations between the adult and the child.

☐ Building Bricks

Toy bricks are very versatile. Among other things, you can make a tower, a train, a bridge or a wall. You can take turns with the child at arranging bricks, or play alongside, using your own set. You can literally build on the child's efforts by showing her new ways of using her bricks.

☐ Nesting beakers

Pile them on top of each other to make a tower. Play a game of 'ready, steady, go' using a large cardboard tube to knock down the tower.

☐ Laser discs

The patterns on these discs are extremely eye-catching. Either spin one on a shiny surface, (turn it as if you were screwing on the lid of a jar, then let go) or hold one in your hand so that it reflects the light.

☐ Action toys

These toys allow the child to take an active role. She will also enjoy taking turns with the adult in making something happen. (Action toys include Jack-in-the-box, pop-up toys, and cause-and-effect toys with levers, buttons and dials.)

☐ Musical instruments

Encourage the child to explore different soundmakers and musical instruments. Allow the child some space and time to initiate her own actions with the soundmaker. You can then follow her lead and help to extend her play by showing her different actions. Choose soundmakers that are visually stimulating, like the Xylophone Roundbells, or a tambourine decorated with ribbons.

Story time

Looking at picture books is a natural way of sharing attention with a child. Encourage children's interest in books by stimulating all their senses:

Books can involve *physical actions* — flaps to lift, tabs to pull, figures to move about. Books can be *tactile* — cloth, fur or sandpaper add texture to the page; Books can be *audible* — some books play a tune, others have bells and buzzers to press. Books can be *olfactory* — look out for books that have 'scratch and sniff' pages. Books can be *three-dimensional* — pop-out books give a three-dimensional effect.

Puzzles

Like books, puzzles are a useful focus for joint activity and talk between the adult and the child. Your tone of voice and facial expression will help build up anticipation as the child attempts to replace a piece. On successful completion, the child's efforts can be rewarded with a clap or a word of praise.

Extend the child's play by using the puzzle in a variety of ways. For example, pieces from an animal puzzle can be used to accompany *Old MacDonald's Farm*; pieces from a shape puzzle can be hidden in a feely bag; and so on.

Look at my puppet

Puppets come alive for children when they have a voice. Animal finger puppets can make animal sounds, people puppets can have squeaky voices. Puppets can be made to dance, sleep, run and jump. Children especially love a naughty puppet. He can steal drinks, knock over bricks and generally be silly.

Mobiles

Hang a sturdy mobile within reach of the child. Encourage her to explore it. Show her how it makes a noise, spins or bounces up and down. Instead of a mobile, use wind chimes or a toy hung on a spring. (See Section 13, *Visual Resources*, for further ideas on things to make.)

Ball games

Roll a ball between you and the child. Encourage her to roll it back, and give her lots of praise if she succeeds. Toys on wheels can be used in a similar way.

Water tray

Join the child at the water tray. You can hold a beaker for her to fill with water, or push a toy boat towards her.

Here are some suggestions for activities and games that involve you and your child looking together:

☐ *My photo album*

Make a photograph album just for your child. This can include pictures of family members, special outings, pets and her own snap shots.

☐ *Peek-a-boo objects*

Play peek-a-boo with various objects, which can disappear behind your back, into a pocket or up a sleeve.

☐ *Jack-in-the-box*

Look for a Jack-in-the-box that has a gentle mechanism. The sudden, forceful movements of certain brands of this toy can be very disturbing for young children. The best types are those that allow your child to both eject Jack and push him back in his box.

☐ *Finger puppet*

A finger puppet is an ideal focus between you and your child, as you can easily keep it within her line of vision. Your child will

enjoy this game even more if she makes a finger puppet for herself. She can then copy your actions. Simply wrap a small piece of material around the finger, and secure it with adhesive tape. Use a washable felt-tip to draw a face on the fingertip.

☐ *My story book*

Keep a few story books as a special treat. (Putting books in a colourful box or smart folder helps signal their importance to the child.) Make a big fuss about bringing them out for you and your child to look at together. You can make the book come alive by acting out the story using objects that match the pictures.

Hide 'n' seek

Play hide 'n' seek games with different objects or favourite toys. Encourage your child to look for them. Use boxes, jars or tins with loose-fitting lids in which to hide small objects.

You can even make up a story for your child to act out by searching for various hidden objects: for example, the story of the little boy who lost his penny and looked in a shoe box and found a teapot; he looked in the teapot and found a jar; he looked in the jar and found some tissue paper; he unwrapped the paper and found the penny.

Feely bag

Hide some objects in an opaque bag with a drawstring neck (an old shoe bag, for instance). Start with three or four items and slowly build up the number. Choose items that have a distinctive texture or shape. Encourage your child to feel an object before she takes it out of the bag. What can she tell you about it?

Here are some suggestions for filling your feely bag: a sponge ball, a doll with a lacy dress, a large wooden cube or brick, wool pompoms, a fir cone, scrunchy paper, cotton wool balls, a bell, a furry soft toy, pebbles, stones and shells, a squeaky toy, a plastic duck, a piece of sandpaper, Christmas cards that have glitter, a soft baby brush, a bunch of keys, a large spoon (metal, wooden or plastic), the plastic tray from inside a biscuit box, a leaf, a feather, a bath sponge, old head bands or bow ties in different materials (velvet, silk, satin, lace).

Down the shoot

Use the tube from the inside of a roll of wrapping paper. Various items can be dropped 'down the shoot'. Try dropping objects into a tin, a bucket, the bath or a sand tray. Accompany the action with suitable noises like 'weee!' and 'plonk!'

Tea party

Have a pretend tea party with your child. Help her lay out the cutlery and plates. Ask her for a cup of tea and a slice of cake. When you finish your tea, ask her for some more!

ALTERNATIVE
Materials & Equipment

The following toys are particularly suitable for developing shared play:

- ☐ Jack-in-the-box
- ☐ books: storybooks, lift the flap, picture, touch and feel, sound and light
- ☐ photo albums
- ☐ construction toys: bricks, Lego, beakers
- ☐ puppets: glove, finger, pop-up
- ☐ puzzles
- ☐ action toys
- ☐ pop-up toys
- ☐ musical instruments: shaker, drum, chime bar, bells, blocks
- ☐ mobiles
- ☐ laser discs

Talk to your child's therapist or teacher about the toys that interest you and your child. Ask them to tick appropriate items from the above list.

SECTION 3

Let's Look Together
CHECKLIST

Child's name	

Date	Activity	Comments
8\8	Book	*Turns pages. Looks intently at the picture for a few seconds*

LOOKING & FOLLOWING

INTRODUCTION ◆ **37**

Teaching Activity   38

Activities for School or Nursery   39

Activities for Home   41

Alternative Materials & Equipment   44

LOOKING & FOLLOWING CHECKLIST ◆ **45**

SECTION 4

INTRODUCTION

THE ABILITY to track an object visually is a major stage in the development of attention skills. It enables the child to sustain attention to an object even when it starts to move out of her field of vision. This is essential if the child is to form adequate concepts about the world. Otherwise, she would not see that a rolling ball knocked down a skittle or that a pathway led to a house. These early tracking skills are a prerequisite to reading, which entails the child being able to scan a line of text.

It is particularly important for looking and following activities that the child is able to turn her head. Some children may have difficulty with balance and head control. In these cases, seek the advice of a physiotherapist on supporting the child's posture.

Looking & Following
TEACHING ACTIVITY
Watch the Puppet

You will need:

a glove puppet

Useful words and phrases:

*puppet, look,
there he/she goes,
here he/she/ comes,
wave bye-bye,
say hello,
where's he gone?*

1 Sit opposite the child at a distance of approximately one metre.

2 Attract the child's attention to the puppet by moving it, making sounds and so on.

3 Once you have the child's attention, start moving the puppet slightly to one side.

4 Stop moving the puppet if the child's attention wanders, and recapture her interest in the same way as before.

5 Repeat the activity, gradually extending the distance each time you move the puppet.

6 When the child is used to the activity, you can make the puppet disappear by moving him behind a screen. The child can be encouraged to watch for him to reappear.

To increase the complexity of the activity

◆ increase the speed of your movements;
◆ change the direction (starting with up-and-down movements, then forwards and backwards, and so on).

Variations

◆ Try using different toys to attract the child's attention.
◆ Let the child hold the puppet. Encourage her to wave it around.

ACTIVITIES FOR
School or Nursery

Here are some suggestions for encouraging children to track moving objects and extend their field of vision. Remember that side-to-side movement is easiest at first, then try up-and-down movement, and finally vary the direction.

☐ Wall frieze

A long wall frieze is one way of encouraging children to follow a sequence of pictures. A picture of a train can be filled with cardboard figures, animals, luggage, and so on. The child will be drawn along the length of the picture by each new image. (Other picture ideas include a bus, plane, caterpillar, dachsund and snake.) For up-and-down tracking, use pictures of a block of flats, a tower, a tall giraffe or a tree complete with birds, fruit and squirrels.

☐ Gallery

Use a wall in a long corridor to make a photo gallery of the children. A special arrangement of the children's pictures can also be included.

☐ Toys that move

Introduce the child to various toys that move along the ground. Try pull-along toys like carts or toys on wheels. Alternate these with items that need to be pushed, like toy cars, trains and aeroplanes. The child will also have fun with radio-controlled vehicles. Show the child how different surfaces affect the movement of the toys. For example, a thick carpet will slow them down, a bumpy surface will make them go up and down, and a downward slope will speed them up.

☐ Slinky

Slinky is a brightly coloured spring available from educational catalogues. Hold the spring horizontally and slowly pull out one side. Once it is fully extended it can be released to spring back into shape. The spring can also be held vertically for the child to track up-and-down movement. (Other similar ideas include unrolling a paper chain or unfurling a banner.)

Where's it gone?

Push toy cars and trains along a track. Once the child is following with the vehicles in sight, you can introduce a tunnel. (These are easy to improvise with an old box, a tube or an open book.) The child can be encouraged to watch for the vehicle to reappear after disappearing into the tunnel.

Marble runs

These toys allow the child to take an active part by dropping the marble into the run. There are numerous commercial varieties available. She will have fun watching the marble rolling along until it pops out at the end.

Footprints

You will need a tray filled with slightly damp sand. Show the child how various objects, for example, the wheels of a toy car or the feet on a plastic doll, make different tracks. Next, make tracks with various items, and then hide them in the sand. The child has to follow the trial to find the hidden item.

Follow the road

This is a particularly good exercise for older children, as it can be used to encourage left-to-right orientation. Draw the outline of a brick road across the page. The child has to colour in each brick across the paper from left to right. Other ideas include a track through a forest, a path to a house, or footprints in the sand.

Skittles

Play a game of skittles. This offers practice in both tracking and hand–eye co-ordination. Empty plastic bottles or cardboard toilet roll holders will serve very well as skittles. This activity can be combined with a listening task by sticking pictures on the skittles. You then name different pictures for the child to hit.

Name game

The children need to stand or sit in a circle for this game. They take it in turns to throw a soft toy or bean bag to another child in the circle. But before they can throw it, they must say the name of the catcher.

Concertina books

Open one page at a time, until the whole book is extended. Alternatively, stick a sequence of object pictures on a long card. The child has to place a matching picture on each one. (You can also obtain concertina books that open downwards, in a vertical direction.)

ACTIVITIES FOR
Home

The following games will help develop your child's ability to follow a moving object. Always attract your child's attention to the object before you begin to move it.

☐ *Roll a ball*

Sit at a small table with your child seated opposite you. You will need a large colourful ball (preferably one with a small bell or rattle inside) to play this game. Attract your child's attention to the ball, then start to roll it slowly from one side of the table to the other. Encourage your child to watch as it drops off the edge.

Position a basket under the table to catch the ball. Your child can then retrieve it for you to repeat the activity.

☐ *Oh blow!*

Collect some small bits of cotton wool or tissue. Place them on a piece of card held between you and the child. Gently blow one towards your child. Can she blow it back again?

☐ *Look up there!*

Balloons and kites prompt the child to look above her. She can also have some control over creating various movement patterns by pulling on the string.

☐ *In the spotlight*

Shine a torch beam along the wall of a darkened room. Talk to your child about any items that are highlighted by the torch. Next, try moving the torch beam up the wall. Let your child have a turn at shining the light around the room. What objects does she pick out with the beam?

☐ *Bubbles*

All children love blowing bubbles. Your child will have to keep track of the bubbles if she wants to pop them.

☐ *Swap a hat*

Sit in front of a large mirror. The idea is to play a dressing up game, but in this version items are swapped between you and the child. Encourage your child to watch in the mirror as you swap clothing.

It's a goal

In this game your child needs to stand between two chairs or in the doorway of the room. You gently kick the ball towards your child. If it gets through the chairs or doorway, you score a goal. To stop the goal, the child needs to watch the rolling ball.

Yo-yo

Playing with a yo-yo is a good way of encouraging your child to track up-and-down movements. Attract your child's attention by using brightly coloured yo-yos that either have a light or make a sound.

Incy-wincy spider

Sing this song to your child. Use your hands to act out the action of the spider slowly climbing up the spout, then tumbling down again. (Other suitable actions songs are *Little Miss Muffet*, *Hoisting up the Sails* and *Hickory Dickory Dock*.)

Pass the parcel

There are several variations of this party game. Traditionally, a parcel is made by wrapping a toy in several layers of paper. The children sit in a circle and pass the parcel quickly from one child to the next. All the time, music is playing. When it stops the child holding the parcel can take off one layer of wrapping paper. The music starts again and the game continues until the toy in the parcel is finally revealed.

Another variation is to have two parcels. One parcel starts off round the circle. It is immediately followed by another. The aim of the game is for the second parcel to overtake the first before it completes one circle. Obviously, the more players you have for this game the better. Instead of parcels, puppets or dolls can be used to represent figures such as a hare and a turtle, a cat and a mouse, a fox and a chicken, or a bird and a worm.

☐ *Animal fun*

A visit to the zoo or local farm will give your child the opportunity to watch animals, birds and fish. Think about all the variety your child will see: the slow crawl of the tortoise, the hopping of a bird, the monkey swinging up in the tree, the quick darting movements of tiny fish, the slow prowl of the big lion. If you have pets, your child can have hours of fun watching the antics of the family cat or dog playing with a ball.

☐ *My book*

Help your child make her own book. Fold stiff paper or card like a concertina to make a pull-out book. Your child can stick photographs or draw pictures on each page. The book can include photographs of your child, the family, pets and favourite toys.

☐ *In the park*

Take your child to the park to see other children hurtling down the slide, swinging high in the sky, whirling in a circle on a roundabout or gently rising up and down on a seesaw.

The following toys and materials encourage looking and following:

Tracking side-to-side and up-and-down

☐ balloons

☐ balls (beach, sponge, ping-pong, Koosh, foam)

☐ bubbles

☐ glove puppets

☐ Slinky

☐ paper chain

☐ banner

Tracking side-to-side

☐ pull-along toys

☐ radio-controlled vehicles

☐ toy cars, buses, planes

☐ wall frieze

☐ concertina books

Tracking up-and-down

☐ yo-yo

☐ toys on a spring or piece of elastic

☐ puppet on a stick

☐ balls on a stick

☐ marble runs

☐ a tall wall poster

Tracking backwards and forwards

☐ skittles

☐ balls (beach, sponge, ping-pong, Koosh, foam)

☐ bubbles

☐ glove puppets

☐ toy cars, buses, planes

☐ wheeled toys

☐ radio-controlled vehicles

See Section 13, *Visual Resources*, for more ideas for objects that have movement.

Talk to your child's therapist or teacher about the materials and activities that interest you and your child. Ask them to tick appropriate items from the above list.

Looking & Following
CHECKLIST

Child's name		

Date	Activity	Comments
26/10	Bubbles	Watches bubbles, but not turning to follow when out of sight

LOOKING AROUND

INTRODUCTION ◆ 49

   Teaching Activity   50

   Activities for School or Nursery   51

   Activities for Home   53

   Alternative Materials & Equipment   55

LOOKING AROUND CHECKLIST ◆ 56

SECTION 5

INTRODUCTION

IN ORDER for children to learn to examine the detail in what they see, they need to have developed some skills in visual scanning. This is the ability actively to search for and assimilate all the visual stimuli that lie within their field of vision. It develops from early visual tracking but is a skill that may not be completely mastered until seven years of age.

The following section has activities designed to encourage the child to explore visually her immediate surroundings. It is particularly important that she is able to turn her head to look. Some children may have difficulty with balance and head control. In these cases, seek the advice of a physiotherapist on supporting the child's posture.

Looking Around
TEACHING ACTIVITY
Match up the Animals

You will need:

several miniature animal pieces

Useful words and phrases:

look, names of animals, where is . . .?

1 Choose three or four animal pieces.

2 Arrange these in a semi-circle, with the pieces fairly close together.

3 Some children find it helpful if you restrict the area for scanning. To do this, place the pieces on a tray or use a hoop to mark out an area.

4 Encourage the child to scan the items by asking her to select one of the pieces. This can be done verbally or non-verbally: you can name an animal; make an animal sound; hold up a duplicate or a picture of one of the animal pieces.

5 Prompt the child by sweeping your hand across the area in which she should be looking. If necessary, point out individual pieces to her.

To increase the complexity of the activity

◆ gradually space the animal pieces farther apart;

◆ space the pieces at random;

◆ gradually increase the number of animal pieces;

◆ introduce pieces that are very similar.

Variations

◆ Place the animals in a model farm, zoo, circus or wild life park.

◆ Set up a doll's house with small family figures.

◆ Use toy vehicles and a garage or street play mat.

ACTIVITIES FOR
School or Nursery

The following activities encourage children to search for and examine all items in their field of vision:

☐ Sand tray

Play this game with two children. One child hides some toys in the sand. The idea is to leave a small part of the toy visible above the sand. The other child has to find them by scanning the tray. (Do not allow the child to just run her hands through the sand.)

☐ Water tray

Put several floatable containers in a large water tray. Can the child find and sink each one by filling it with water?

☐ Find the animal

Use imaginative play with miniature animals and a toy farm to encourage visual scanning. (Remember to check that children are familiar with animal names before you start.) You can name animals for the children to find or encourage pretend play by asking them to relate items to each other. Requests might include "Where's the pig?", "Make the duck swim in the pond" or "Put the farmer next to the horse". Use plastic animals that vary in colour and position. You can ask the child to find "the cow lying down" or "the brown horse". This will encourage the child to scan several different pieces until she finds the correct one. (Other ideas are animals at a zoo, circus or wild life park.)

☐ Looking corner

Set up a looking corner. Use various displays to encourage the children to look at items in detail, as well as scanning a large group of items. (See Section 1, *Look and Learn*, for more ideas on displays for looking corners.)

☐ Library

Encourage children to search for their favourite books in the book corner.

☐ Where's the picture?

Stick several large pictures on the wall. Give the child a duplicate of one of the pictures. Can she point to the matching one on the wall?

☐ Find the matching pair

Draw rows of similar objects on a sheet of paper. Remember to work on one attribute at a time. This could be colour, shape, pattern or a mixture: for example, a series of oval footballs could be plain, spotted, striped or chequered. Make two of them identical. Ask the child to find the two that match. (Start with two plain, as this will be easier for the child.)

☐ Picture lotto

Lotto games encourage children to scan several pictures. Games that encourage children to match object pictures to a composite picture containing the same objects are also very useful.

ACTIVITIES FOR
Home

The following activities will encourage your child to search out visually interesting items in her surroundings:

☐ *Looking board*

Make a looking board for your child. You will need a cork notice board and several sticky-backed hooks. Attach the hooks to the board at well-spaced intervals. Help your child to hang different objects on the board, such as Christmas baubles, a bunch of keys or an unusual earring. Hang the board where your child can easily see it, but out of reach. (It is probably better if you supervise your child in touching and handling the objects.) The objects can be changed regularly so that your child is encouraged to look at the board.

☐ *Looking poster*

Cut out pictures from magazines and stick these on a large sheet of paper. Choose colourful pictures and cut round the outline of objects to make them more eye-catching. Spend some time looking at the poster with your child.

☐ *Fridge magnets*

Arrange your magnets at well-spaced intervals on the front of your fridge or freezer. (Remember to place them where your child can see them.) Encourage your child to look at each one. She can help you choose the next one you buy.

☐ Doll's house

Join your child when she is playing with her doll's house. Show her some actions with the dolls, and then ask her to carry out a similar action. You can put the baby doll to bed, and then ask her to make the man doll go to sleep. (Other games that involve imaginative play with several items can be played in a similar way: for example, vehicles in a garage, animals on a toy farm, or toy figures like *Power Rangers*.)

☐ Pretend shops

Use tins and packets of food to play a game of pretend shops. Spread the items out on a table or the floor. Give your child a shopping bag and ask her to fetch one item at a time for you. You can gradually increase the number of items on your shopping list. Let your child send you to the shops. She will still have to scan the items to deside what she needs.

☐ Look 'n' cook

Ask your child to fetch you ingredients from the cupboard or fridge. Encourage her to look carefully along the shelves, including those above and below her immediate eye-level.

☐ Search the hangers

Ask your child to find certain items of clothing. Encourage her to stand back and look for the item, rather than searching through hanger by hanger. You can play the same game by looking for items in the airing cupboard.

☐ Treasure hunt

Tell your child you are going to hide some treasure in one of the cupboards or drawers in your living room. The treasure can be anything from sweets to a toy or a balloon. She will have to find the special sign that marks the hiding place. Stick a cardboard star to mark where you have hidden the treasure.

ALTERNATIVE
Materials & Equipment

The following toys encourage scanning:

- [ ] multi-piece puzzles or jigsaws
- [ ] small doll material: doll's house garage
- [ ] *Playmobile* play sets
- [ ] miniature animals: farm zoo circus
- [ ] picture posters
- [ ] large busy pictures
- [ ] picture lotto games

Talk to your child's therapist or teacher about the materials and activities that interest you and your child. Ask them to tick appropriate items from the above list.

SECTION 5

Looking Around
CHECKLIST

Child's name	

Date	Activity	Comments
19/11	Pretend shops	*Looks at items in the middle of a line, but needs prompting to look at each end*

VISUAL MATCHING

Introduction ◆ 59

COLOUR ◆ 60

Teaching Activity 60
Activities for School or Nursery 61
Activities for Home 64
Alternative Materials & Equipment 66

SIZE: BIG & SMALL ◆ 67

Teaching Activity 67
Activities for School or Nursery 68
Activities for Home 70

SIZE: LONG & SHORT ◆ 72

Activities for School or Nursery 72
Activities for Home 73
Alternative Materials & Equipment 74

SHAPE ◆ 75

Teaching Activity 75
Activities for School or Nursery 76
Activities for Home 79

VISUAL MATCHING CHECKLIST ◆ 82

SECTION 6

INTRODUCTION

VISUAL MATCHING is the first step towards more complex visual tasks such as sorting. It requires the child to recognize when two objects share one or more characteristics. This helps to develop the child's understanding of different concepts like colour, size and shape.

Use these activities to build up the child's perceptual skills. Alternatively, incorporate the games into an attention training programme.

You will need:

several red bricks,
several yellow bricks,
a red plate and
a yellow plate

**Useful words
and phrases:**

look, red, yellow,
same, different,
plate, brick

1 Take two red bricks and show them to the child. Talk about how they are the same.

2 Let the child keep one brick and take away the other. Place a red plate in view on the table. First let the child watch as you place your brick on the plate and then encourage her to do the same with hers.

3 Bring out another pair of bricks and again place your brick on the plate and encourage the child to do the same with hers.

4 Repeat this with several other red bricks until the child is imitating spontaneously.

5 Now try with one red brick and one yellow brick. Give the red brick to the child and keep the yellow one. Bring out the yellow plate and place your brick on it. Encourage the child to place her brick on the red plate.

6 Repeat step 5 until the child is consistent in placing her red bricks on the plate.

7 When you feel the child is ready, give her a yellow brick, and encourage her to place it on the yellow plate. Continue the activity, alternating between red and yellow bricks.

To increase the complexity of the activity

◆ remove the plates and ask the child to match brick to brick;

◆ increase the number of colours;

◆ use non-identical objects, for example, red car, red spoon, red button.

Variations

◆ Use the bricks to build a tower, make a train or lay a road.

◆ Stack beakers together according to colour.

◆ Thread beads to make necklaces and bracelets.

Colour

ACTIVITIES FOR
School or Nursery

The following games encourage the child to match items by colour. At this stage the child should only be required to match one object with another.

☐ Tidy boxes

Use different coloured containers to store items by colour: for example, a red crayon in a red box, a blue crayon in a blue box. Give the child one item at a time to put away.

☐ Find the clown's balloon

Make a large picture of a clown and stick this on the wall. One hand of the clown should be reaching out and holding onto several pieces of string that lead to coloured cut-outs of balloons. Collect together several balloons with colours that match the cut-outs.

The children are asked to select a balloon and blow it up. When they have matched it to the appropriate cut-out, they can tie it to the wall by the string.

☐ Team-up by colour

In sports and games lessons, use colour to mark the different teams. The children select a sash from an assortment of colours. The children must form into groups according to the colour of their sashes.

☐ Match the object to the table

Use three different coloured pieces of crepe paper to cover separate tables. Have ready a selection of coloured objects. Each child takes it in turn to match an object to the table with the appropriate colour.

☐ Find the colour walk

Choose one child at time to go on a colour walk. Hand her an object in one colour and ask her to find other objects of the same colour around the room. Make this into a game by allowing each child to go once round the room to collect as many matching objects as they can. The winner is the one with the most objects.

☐ Colour table

Show the children a colour. Ask them to find objects with the same colour. Display the children's collection on a table.

☐ Print a colour

You will need two identical solid geometric shapes and some red and yellow paint for printing. Use the red paint to print a shape on one piece of paper. Then use the yellow paint to print a shape on a different piece of paper. Let each child have a turn at printing a shape. They have to choose a colour then match it to the correct picture.

☐ Hit a colour

You will need different coloured balls and different coloured hoops. (Wrap crepe paper around the hoop.) The children must hit the ball through the hoops with the same colour.

☐ Colour hoop-la

You will need different coloured hoops and different coloured pegs. The children must throw a hoop onto a matching peg. (Instead of pegs you could use coloured cardboard boxes or plastic tidy baskets with either hoops or bean bags.)

☐ Colour dice

Use colour dice with board games to see who has the next turn. (Give each child a colour card or use a coloured token for the board game.)

☐ Colour marks the route

Mark out routes around the nursery or school using large colour footprints. The child is given a colour and asked to follow the route. Make it more fun by having several different routes crossing over each other.

☐ Colour coded

Choose children by the colour of their clothes; for example, all those wearing red can line up first for dinner. Remember to hold up the colour so the task is a matching one and not a comprehension one.

☐ Colour pairs

Each child in a group is given a different coloured bag. Have several different coloured objects hidden in a box. Take one out at a time. The child who has the matching colour puts up her hand, and is allowed to put the object into her bag. (Alternatively, use coloured flower pots, beakers, baskets, card or mats.)

☐ Colour dominoes

Instead of matching up numbers, these dominoes have colour. Make some simple dominoes from stiff card and coloured gummed paper. (Or use cotton reels painted half in one colour and half in another. The child threads the reels onto a shoelace.)

☐ Pop-up colour puppets

Each child wears a different coloured finger puppet. These can be made from material or paper. Ask the children to hide their puppets under the table. Bring out different coloured objects. The child with the matching colour must pop up her puppet.

These games will help your child to recognize when two colours are the same. Always show the child the colour for the matching game.

☐ *Find a pair*

Use household items and clothing to play a matching game. Give her one of the pair and see if she can find the other. In the bathroom she can match a red toothbrush to a red beaker, a yellow flannel to a yellow towel. In the kitchen she can match a blue cup to a blue saucer, a yellow plate to a yellow-handled knife. In the bedroom she can match a green sock to a green shoe, and a brown glove to a brown hat.

☐ *Colour scrapbook*

Help your child find pictures to stick in a scrapbook. Start with two colours: for example, red on one page and green on the other. She has to find the right page for her picture. Make several books using different colour combinations.

☐ *Post a colour*

Collect together objects in two different colours. Label two cardboard boxes or two plastic sweet jars with the same colours. Hand one object at a time to the child for her to post. To make it more interesting, your child can drop the objects down a cardboard tube into the jar.

☐ *Colour snap*

Stick coloured, gummed paper onto cards. When two players turn over cards with the same colour, the first to shout "snap!" gets to keep the cards.

☐ *Making jewellery*

Beads and threading strings are sold in most toy shops, or you could use coloured buttons and a shoe lace. Start making a necklace with beads in one colour. Help your child to thread some beads. When you have threaded several beads, start another necklace in a different colour. Again help your child to thread some beads, using the new colour. Next, bring out a bead and see if your child can choose the necklace with the matching beads. (Try making bracelets, rings or belts.)

Colour lotto

Make a coloured lotto by sticking six squares of gummed paper onto a large piece of card. Make six cards to match the squares. Give your child one card at a time to match to the squares. (Instead of cards, use coloured objects.)

Object pairs

Collect together objects that match each other in colour: for example, a red toy car and a red pencil, a blue scarf and a blue brick, a yellow button and a yellow toothbrush. Help your child put the matching pairs together. Make the game more interesting by hiding one matching set in a feely bag.

Hunt for this colour

Give your child one coloured object. Ask her to find similar coloured items from around the room.

I see colour

When going for a walk, take with you a coloured card or piece of coloured material. Point out colours around you that match the card or the material. Encourage your child to join in the game. On an 'I see red' walk, you might see a red car, knock on a red door, look up at a red flag, meet a friend wearing a red jumper or smell a red rose.

Collect a colour

Collect items in one colour to bring home. A green collection might include a small green leaf, a crisp green apple, a leaflet printed with green ink, a blade of grass, a piece of moss or an acorn that has fallen out of the tree.

Colour poster

Cut out pictures from magazines of items that are the same colour. Help your child stick these on a large poster.

Point to the colour

Look at a picture or poster where there are lots of people and objects in different colours. Show your child one colour. Ask her to point out things in the picture that have the same colour.

ALTERNATIVE
Materials & Equipment

Choose items for colour matching from the following types of materials:

☐ everyday objects		☐ material	
☐ doll-size items		☐ plastic shapes	
☐ miniature items		☐ toy vehicles	
☐ toys		☐ Plasticine	
☐ household items		☐ paints, crayons or pencils	
☐ clothes		☐ decorations	
☐ food			
☐ paper			

Talk to your child's therapist or teacher about the materials that interest you and your child. Ask them to tick appropriate items from the above list.

Big & Small
TEACHING ACTIVITY

Size

1 Choose one big cup and one small cup. Place them in front of the child, allowing her to touch as well as look at them.

2 Bring out another big cup. Draw the child's attention to the similarity in size of the two larger cups. Place the two objects together.

3 Bring out a small cup and ask the child to place it with the other small one.

4 Repeat steps 1–3 using different object pairs.

5 Now the child is ready to try making a choice when matching. Put a big and a small cup on the table. Bring out a big cup. Can the child place it with the other big cup?

6 If the child has difficulty in matching up the pair, encourage her to hold the cup next to the ones on the table. Continue with other object pairs.

To increase the complexity of the activity

◆ increase the number of object pairs presented to the child;

◆ make the size difference smaller;

◆ introduce non-identical pairs.

Variations

◆ Ask the child to place big objects in a big box and small objects in a small box.

◆ Use pictures of objects.

The above teaching activity can be adapted to teach the concepts of long and short, and thick and thin. See Section 13, *Visual Resources*, for suitable materials.

You will need:

several pairs of identical objects in various sizes, such as two large cups, two miniature cups

Useful words and phrases:

look, same, different, big, small/little

S E C T I O N 6

The following games encourage the child to match items by size. At this stage the child should only be required to match one object with another.

☐ *Footprints and handprints*

Make footprints and handprints, either in paint or in sand. Can the child find a print that matches her own size?

☐ *Tidy by size*

Store items according to their size: for example, big bricks in one box, small bricks in another. Give the child one item at a time to put away.

☐ *Collect a miniature*

Ask the children to collect one miniature object each. Make a matchbox collection and put this on display. The group can compare the different items in the collection.

☐ *Size table*

Collect large and small objects for a size table. Place a large object to one side of the table, and a small object to the other side. Let the children take it in turns to place an object on the table. The aim is to have similar-sized objects grouped together.

☐ *Size lotto*

Collect together pairs of objects that are identical except for size. Make several lotto cards with pictures representing the objects. (Try not to have pictures of both objects in a pair on the same card.) Give each child a lotto card, then show the children one object at a time. The child with the matching picture puts up her hand. If she is correct, she can place the object on her lotto board.

Match the objects

In this game each child selects an object from a bag. Then they are shown a tray with matching objects. Each child must choose the one that matches her own size. (Be careful to have a variety of sizes for each object, so that the child has to match for size and not just identify her object.)

Picture pairs

Make some picture cards depicting a large item on one half, and a small item on the other half. For example, a big book and a little book. Cut the cards in half. Use the picture halves to play a pairs game.

Teddy bear's tea party

You will need one small bear and one large bear with a tea service in both miniature and doll sizes. Take one piece out at a time, and ask the child to match it to either the large or the small bear.

A similar game can be played using clothing. In this game the child is helped by the fact that the clothes will only fit the right-sized bear. Clothes for a holiday can be packed away in either a large or a small suitcase.

Moving day

You will need one large and one small cardboard box with furniture in both doll and miniature sizes. Take one piece out at a time, and ask the child to match it to either the large or the small box. (Alternatively, you can use a large and small toy van or a large and small doll's house.)

Size: Big & Small
ACTIVITIES FOR
Home

These games will help your child to recognize when two objects are the same size.

☐ *Exploring size*

Encourage your child to explore the size of different objects, for example comparing two differently sized objects by holding one in each hand, or trying to fit different objects first into a small box and then into a big box.

☐ *Tidy up by size*

Encourage your child to help you store things according to size. Remember to start her off by separating items according to size, and then giving her one item at a time. In the kitchen she can stack cups, plates and dishes by size, and divide spoons into tablespoons, dessertspoons and teaspoons. In the airing cupboard socks, vests and pants can be folded into different piles. Likewise, scarves, hats and gloves can be arranged by size. She can also tidy her toys by size, so that big dolls go on one shelf, and little dolls go on another.

☐ *Match up the biscuit*

Enlist your child's help in making some round biscuits in a variety of sizes. When they are baked, she can match up pairs of biscuits by size, and then join them with icing to make a custard cream.

☐ *Size scrapbook*

Cut out pictures of big and small items. Help your child stick these into a scrapbook. Keep big objects on one page, and small objects on another. You could have animals with their young; big and small pictures of the same object (like a teaspoon and a dessertspoon); or pictures of a variety of big and small items (such as a thimble, a pin or a button and an elephant, a house or a tree). Start your child off by sticking a big and a small picture in the book. Give her another picture and see if she can match it with a similar sized one.

Post it by size

Collect together objects in two sizes. You will also need two cardboard boxes or two plastic sweet jars, one large and one small. Show your child how to post an object in each box, then hand her an object for her to post. To make it more interesting, your child can drop objects down a cardboard tube into the jar.

Match this size

Show your child an object. Help her to find objects that are the same size. Lay all the objects out in a line so that she is more able to compare sizes. Alternatively, show her how a small key or coin fits in a matchbox. Ask her to find other items that will fit in the box.

My little shoe

Show your child one adult size shoe and one of her own shoes. Hand her another big shoe. Let her try the shoe on and talk about how it doesn't fit. Can she match it with the other big shoe? Bring out more big and small shoes for her to match.

Size scrap poster

Help your child cut out several pictures of big and small versions of the same item: for example, two dessertspoons and three teaspoons. Stick the pictures on a large poster. Point to one picture and see if your child can find another one in a similar size.

The following games encourage the child to match items by length. At this stage the child should only be required to match one object with another.

☐ *Tidy by length*

Store items according to their length: for example, long pencils in one box, short pencils in another. Give the child one item at a time to put away.

☐ *Long and short display*

Collect long and short items to hang on the wall. Attach one long item to the wall and then, a little farther away, a short item. Let the children take it in turns to hang up the remaining items. The aim is to have items of a similar length hanging together.

☐ *Size lotto*

Collect together pairs of objects that are identical except for length. Make several lotto cards with pictures representing the objects. (Try not to have pictures of both objects in a pair on the same card.) Give each child a lotto card, then show the children one object at a time. The child with the matching picture puts up her hand. If she is correct, she can place the object on her lotto board.

☐ *Match the objects*

In this game each child selects an object from a bag. Then they are shown a tray with matching objects. Each child must choose the one that matches her own in length. (Be careful to have a variety of lengths for each object, so that the child has to match for size and not just identify her object.)

☐ *Line up your pegs*

Put two rows of pegs in a pegboard. Make one long and the other short. Can the child copy the rows?

Size: Long & Short

ACTIVITIES FOR
Home

These games will help your child to recognize when two objects are the same length.

☐ **Make me a snake**

Use Plasticine to make a long and a short snake. Give your child some Plasticine and ask her to copy either the long or the short snake.

☐ **Colour in my drawing**

Draw a long row of squares and a short row of squares. Make a model of one of the rows using wooden bricks or Lego. Ask your child to colour in the drawing that is the same length as your bricks.

☐ **Match this length**

Show your child an object. Help her to find objects that are similar in length. Lay all the objects out in a line so that she is more able to compare sizes.

☐ **Long and short scrap poster**

Help your child cut out several pictures of long and short versions of the same item: for example, two long scarves and one short scarf. Stick the pictures on a large poster. Point to one picture and see if your child can find another one of a similar length.

These activities can be adapted to work on 'Thick & Thin'. Look at Section 13, *Visual Resources*, for ideas on suitable materials.

You may carry out similar activities with a variety of equipment, such as the following:

- ☐ everyday objects
- ☐ doll-size items
- ☐ miniature items
- ☐ household items
- ☐ clothes
- ☐ picture material
- ☐ cardboard or plastic templates

Talk to your child's therapist or teacher about the materials that interest you and your child. Ask them to tick appropriate items from the above list.

Shape
TEACHING ACTIVITY

Thread a Shape

1. Start making a necklace by threading the spherical beads onto one of the laces.

2. Encourage the child to help you thread the beads.

3. When you have threaded several beads, put the necklace to one side.

4. Start another necklace with the cube-shaped beads. Again encourage the child to thread some beads.

5. When you have threaded several beads, bring out the other necklace and lay both of them in front of the child.

6. Give the child a bead and see if she can choose the necklace with the matching beads.

7. Let her feel the smoothness of the sphere compared with the sharp edges of the cube. It may also help her if the bead is held against each of the necklaces in order to make a visual comparison.

8. Continue until all of the beads are threaded.

To increase the complexity of the activity

◆ introduce different shapes;

◆ introduce less familiar shapes;

◆ introduce shapes that are very similar.

Variations

◆ Make bracelets and belts.

◆ Ask the child to put pairs of beads together that have matching shapes.

◆ Ask the child to put the spherical beads in a round box, and the cube-shaped beads in a square box.

You will need:

several beads in the shape of cubes, several beads in the shape of spheres, two laces for threading

Useful words and phrases:

look, same, different, round, square, necklace, next one

SECTION 6

The following games encourage the child to match items by shape. Remember that matching identical objects is easier for the child than matching three-dimensional objects to a template or drawing.

Shape table

Show the children a shape. Ask them to bring in an object from home that has the same shape. Display the children's collection on a table.

Match the shape

In this game each child selects an object from a bag. They are then shown a tray with matching objects. Each child must choose the one that matches her own in shape. (Be careful to have a variety of shapes for each object, so that the child has to match for shape and not just identify her object; for example, a square, round and rectangular alarm clock.)

A shape marks the spot

If you are working with a small group of children, you can use shapes to help identify personal spaces. Mark each child's coat peg or chair with a black piece of paper cut into a square, circle or other shape. The child is given a matching cut-out of the shape to help her find her coat and chair. Change the shapes on a regular basis. (If you have a large group, use shape, colour and size together. So you may have large or small red, blue and green circles.)

Musical shapes

Play this game in a large hall. On each wall place a large outline of a shape. Ask the children to march around the hall while you play some music. Explain that you will stop the music and hold up a shape. The children must run and stand under the matching shape on the wall. Anyone in the wrong place is out of the game.

Shapes all around us

Show the children a shape. Choose one child at a time to find an object in the room that has the same shape. Make this into a game by allowing each child to go once round the room to collect as many matching objects as she can. The winner is the one with the most objects.

Shapes in drawings

Draw outlines of buildings, vehicles, everyday objects and so on, using different shapes. A house may have a triangle for a roof, a square for the main shape, and rectangles for doors and windows. Let each child have a turn at sticking a matching shape onto an outline.

Leaf shapes

Place a variety of leaves on a large sheet of white paper. Spray over the leaves with paint so that when the leaf is removed an outline is left. Ask the children to match the leaves to the correct outlines. Alternatively, use leaf rubbings or leaf prints.

Object prints

Try the above activity using a variety of everyday objects: for example, a coin, a key or a comb.

Find your biscuit

Give each child a paper serviette folded into a square, rectangle or triangle. The children must choose a biscuit whose shape matches their serviette. (Tins of biscuit assortments have a variety of shapes.)

Print a shape

You will need a toy brick, a round lid from a jar and some blue paint. Print some blue squares using the brick on one piece of paper. Then use the lid to print some blue circles on a different piece of paper. Let each child have a turn at printing a shape. They have to choose a shape then match it to the correct picture.

Trace a shape

Use different templates to trace a variety of shapes. Can the children match the templates to the shapes?

Crack the code

Give the children a code to 'crack' using shapes. They must find the hidden treasure by following a trail. The secret to discovering the trail is to find the shapes that mark where the clues are hidden. For instance, you might place a circle on a box that contains either a written clue or an object like a key or signpost. Remember to show the children the shape before they start searching. (To make this game harder, you can hide clues under an object that has a similar shape. So, for a circle, the clue would be hidden under a round clock.)

Shape pairs

Each child in a group is given a different card with the outline of a shape. Have several different-shaped objects hidden in a box. Take one out at a time. The child who has the matching shape card puts up her hand, and is allowed to put the object on her card. (You can have as many objects as you like, as long as you only present the child with one at a time.)

Shapes first

You will need an assortment of templates. Let the children select one template each. From this basic shape, they have to draw a picture. For instance, a circle becomes a face, a square becomes a house. The children can look at each other's pictures and discuss the shapes that have been used. Can they match the templates to the correct drawings?

Spot the shape

Show the child a composite picture, for example a picture of a family in the garden. Give the child a shape. Can she find objects in the picture that have the same shape?

Shape dominoes

Instead of matching up numbers, these dominoes have shapes. Make some simple dominoes from stiff card. Draw the outline of various shapes with a black felt-tip.

Shape
ACTIVITIES FOR
Home

These games will help your child to recognize when two shapes are the same.

☐ Make a shape

Show your child how to make shapes from Plasticine, dough or pastry. Can she match the pastry cutters to the shapes she has made? Help her by giving her one shape at a time to match to one of a pair of pastry cutters.

☐ Post a shape

Collect together objects in two shapes. Use paper shapes that match the objects to label two cardboard boxes or two plastic sweet jars. Hand one object at a time to your child to post in the box or jar. To make it more interesting, your child can drop the objects down a cardboard tube into the box or jar.

☐ Shape poster

Collect together odds and ends to make a shape poster. A rectangular poster might have a bus ticket, a leaflet, a chocolate bar wrapper and an envelope. Encourage your child to trace the outline of the items.

☐ Lay the table

Lay one table setting for dinner. The child has to copy the place setting for the rest of the family.

☐ Make a sandwich

Enlist your child's help in making sandwiches in different shapes: for example, cut a slice of bread diagonally to make two triangles: across the middle to make two rectangles or use a pastry cutter to make two circles. Ask your child to match up the pieces of bread to make a round sandwich, a triangular sandwich and so on.

☐ Shape scrapbook

Draw a shape for your child. Can she find pictures of similarly shaped objects in a magazine or catalogue? Let her cut out the pictures and stick them in a scrapbook. Repeat, using a different shape.

Shape snap

Cut out shapes from gummed paper and stick these onto cards. Play snap: the first player to shout "Snap!" when two matching cards are turned over gets to keep the cards. Make the game harder by using shapes in different colours. The cards have to match in both colour and shape.

Pack the case

Cut out pictures of items with different shapes from a catalogue: for example, a round cushion, a rectangular book, a square clock. Next, draw a large suitcase containing outlines of various shapes. The child has to pack the items in the suitcase by matching up the shapes. Alternatively, you can draw a series of boxes — round, square, oval or rectangular. The child has pictures of several items to fit into the boxes: for example, a round hat, a box of tissues, a book and an oval pie dish.

Shape lotto

Make a shape lotto by cutting out six shapes and sticking them onto a large piece of card. Make six cards that match the shapes. Give your child one card at a time to match to a shape. (Instead of cards, you could use differently shaped objects that match those on the lotto card.)

Object pairs

Collect together objects that match each other in shape: for example, a square book and a square picture, a round clock and a round plate, a rectangular pencil case and a rectangular notepad. (Keep the pairs fairly similar in size.) Help your child to pair up the items. Make the game more interesting by hiding one matching set in a feely bag.

Find this shape

Give your child an object. Ask her to find similar-shaped items from around the room.

I see a shape

Take your child for a walk. Show her a shape and then point out any matching shapes that you see. Encourage her to join in the game. On an 'I see something round' walk, you might carry a balloon, kick a ball, meet a friend wearing a round badge or jump on a round drainhole cover.

Collect items in one shape to bring home. A square collection might include a badge, a box, a leaflet and a book from the library.

Shape
ALTERNATIVE
Materials & Equipment

The following materials are useful for shape-matching activities:

☐ three-dimensional solid geometric shapes

☐ beads

☐ Plasticine, dough or pastry shapes

☐ plastic shapes from construction toys

☐ cardboard or plastic templates

☐ puzzle pieces

☐ gummed paper shapes

☐ stencils

☐ boxes

Talk to your child's therapist or teacher about the materials that interest you and your child. Ask them to tick appropriate items from the above list.

© Diana Williams 1998
You may photocopy this page for instructional use only

Visual Matching
CHECKLIST

Child's name	

Date	Activity	Comments
28/2	Matching shapes	Able to match circle and square

P

VISUAL SORTING

Introduction ◆ 85

COLOUR　　　　　　　　　　　　　　　　◆ 86

Teaching Activity　　　　　　　　　　　86
Activities for School or Nursery　　　87
Activities for Home　　　　　　　　　89
Alternative Materials & Equipment　91

SIZE: BIG & SMALL　　　　　　　　◆ 92

Teaching Activity　　　　　　　　　　　92
Activities for School or Nursery　　　93
Activities for Home　　　　　　　　　95

SIZE: LONG & SHORT　　　　　　◆ 97

Activities for School or Nursery　　　97
Activities for Home　　　　　　　　　98
Alternative Materials & Equipment　99

SHAPE　　　　　　　　　　　　　　　◆ 100

Teaching Activity　　　　　　　　　　100
Activities for School or Nursery　　101
Activities for Home　　　　　　　　103
Alternative Materials & Equipment　105

ADVANCED SORTING ACTIVITIES　◆ 106

VISUAL SORTING CHECKLIST　　◆ 107

SECTION 7

INTRODUCTION

VISUAL SORTING requires the child to recognize that items within a group have similarities. The child is then able to sort these items according to this likeness. The child begins to learn that objects can be grouped together because of a number of shared attributes like colour, shape and size. Later on the child will learn how to classify items on a conceptual level, using characteristics like function to identify a class of objects.

Children should be able to match items visually before attempting these sorting activities. This is where the child has to identify whether two items are the same, as opposed to sorting a group of items. (See Section 6 for more activities on visual matching.)

Colour
TEACHING ACTIVITY
Colour Bricks

You will need:

*several red bricks,
several blue bricks,
a red tray and a blue tray*

**Useful words
and phrases:**

*look, red, blue, tray,
sort, same, different*

1 Place the two trays on the table. Give the child a red brick to place in the red tray. Next, give her a blue brick to place in the blue tray.

2 When she has succeeded in matching the bricks to the trays, you can try a sorting task.

3 Place three or four red and blue bricks in front of the child. Ask her to sort them into the right trays.

4 Gradually increase the number of bricks the child has to sort.

To increase the complexity of the activity

◆ increase the number of colours;
◆ use plain trays for sorting;
◆ sort the bricks without the trays;
◆ ask the child to sort the bricks without demonstrating the task first.

Variations

◆ Use the bricks to build towers, trains or long snakes.
◆ Ask the child to post the bricks into a box or jar.
◆ Use the beads or counters instead of bricks.

Colour

ACTIVITIES FOR
School or Nursery

The following games provide practice in sorting items according to their colour. There are ideas for both group and individual work.

Build a tower

Give the child a box of coloured wooden bricks. Ask her to build a red tower, a yellow tower and so on. You may need to place the first few bricks to get her started. (Lego can be used in a similar way.)

Sort away by colour

Use coloured containers to store items by colour. For example, give the child several coloured crayons to sort by colour and place in the appropriate containers.

Sort and thread

Provide some threading laces, with coloured beads or cotton reels. (Both these items are available from educational catalogues.) The child must sort and then thread the beads or reels. The idea is to have several laces in different colours.

Jewellery beads

Ask the child to sort coloured beads for necklaces, bracelets, rings and so on. Give the child beads in one shape, and only ask her to sort by colour. (Use an old trinket box with drawers as a sorting box.)

It's a knock-out

You will need a large coloured box for each team, and a large number of inflated balloons in matching colours. Place the balloons in baskets in the middle of the room. (One basket per team.) Each team is given a set time to collect balloons for their box. The winners are the team with the most balloons in their box. (Variations could include only letting the children use one hand or having to blow the balloons up as well.)

Sort and match

You will need a variety of coloured counters and a long strip of white card. Use a black felt-tip to mark out several rows of circles on the card. They should be a similar size to the counters. Place a different coloured counter at the beginning of each row. The child must sort the counters and complete the rows. (The rows could be part of a pathway leading to a house. So a red pathway leads to a house with a red door, and so on.)

Decorate a cake

Ask the children to sort out cake decorations by colour: for example, red decorations for a cherry cake, brown decorations for a chocolate cake, and so on.

Object sort

You will need plastic tidy baskets in a variety of colours. Collect together coloured objects that are small or medium in size. Ask a group of children to sort the objects into the baskets.

Colour

ACTIVITIES FOR
Home

The following games provide your child with practice at sorting a group of items according to their colour:

☐ *Colour-coded wardrobe*

Ask your child to sort out her clothes according to their colour. Start her off by putting out one item of clothing in each of the colours. Give her a bundle of clothes to sort into different piles.

☐ *My sorting box*

Keep different coloured items in a box for your child to sort. They could include buttons, crayons, pencils, straws, scraps of material or assorted objects, such as toy cars and balls. Make some colour cards by sticking squares of gummed paper onto stiff white card. Ask your child to place items from her sorting box onto the appropriate colour card.

☐ *Straws in a beaker*

You will need some coloured straws and several coloured beakers for this game. Match a straw to each of the beakers. Encourage your child to continue until all the straws have been placed in the beakers.

☐ *Button box*

Collect together some coloured buttons for your child to sort. These can be threaded onto a shoe lace or pipe cleaner according to their colour. Remember to knot the lace or bend the pipe cleaner, so the buttons do not fall off.

☐ *Sort a picture*

Cut out from magazines and catalogues pictures of items in different colours. Give them to your child for sorting. She can stick the pictures in a scrapbook. Have one colour per page.

☐ *Colour wash*

Let your child help you sort your washing. Can she separate the whites from the coloureds? Can she sort out the different colours?

☐ Pack by colour

Draw several large suitcases, boxes and bags in different colours. Help your child cut out coloured items from magazines and catalogues. Mix up the pictures and then ask your child to sort them into the different bags according to their colour.

☐ My sorting envelope

Cut out several circles from different coloured card or stick gummed paper onto white card. Keep the cut-outs in an envelope. Your child can take them out and sort them into different piles.

Colour

ALTERNATIVE
Materials & Equipment

Choose items for colour sorting from the following types of materials:

- ☐ everyday objects
- ☐ doll-size items
- ☐ miniature items
- ☐ toys
- ☐ household items
- ☐ clothes
- ☐ food
- ☐ paper

- ☐ material
- ☐ plastic shapes
- ☐ toy vehicles
- ☐ Plasticine
- ☐ paints, crayons or pencils
- ☐ decorations

Talk to your child's therapist or teacher about the materials that interest you and your child. Ask them to tick appropriate items from the above list.

Size: Big & Small
TEACHING ACTIVITY
Sorting by Size

several small red bricks, several large red bricks and a box that will hold the brick

Useful words and phrases:

look, same, different, large/big, small/little

1 Put the bricks in the box and mix the two sizes together.

2 Choose one big brick and one small brick. Place them in front of the child, allowing her to touch as well as look at them.

3 Bring out another big brick. Draw the child's attention to the similarity in size of the two larger bricks. Place the two bricks together.

4 Bring out a small brick and ask the child to place it with the other small one.

5 Next give the child one big and one small brick. Ask her to place them with the other. If she has difficulty, encourage her to hold the bricks next to the ones on the table.

6 Once the child has managed step 5, she is ready to try sorting the remaining bricks. Give her the box and ask her to sort the bricks into big and small bricks.

To increase the complexity of the activity

◆ make the size difference smaller;

◆ introduce non-identical pairs;

◆ ask the child to sort the bricks without demonstrating the task first.

Variations

◆ Ask the child to sort the big bricks into a big box and the small bricks into a small box.

◆ Use the bricks to build a big tower and a small tower.

◆ Give the child lots of large and small Lego bricks to sort. Ask her to build a house using the large pieces of Lego and a house using the small pieces of Lego. Talk about the differences in size of the two houses.

The above teaching activity can be adapted to teach the concepts of long and short, and thick and thin. See Section 13, *Visual Resources*, for suitable materials.

Size: Big & Small

ACTIVITIES FOR
School or Nursery

The following games provide practice in sorting items according to their size. There are ideas for both group and individual work.

☐ Sort and display sizes

Ask the children to collect different-sized objects for a size table. The children must group objects together that are the same size.

☐ Sort and tidy

Store items by size. Give the children several items to tidy away: for example, big bricks in one box, small bricks in another.

☐ Sort the pairs

Collect pairs of objects that are identical except for their size. Keep the pairs in a box. Ask the child to sort the objects into two jars: one jar for the larger size and one jar for the smaller size.

☐ Teddy bear's tea party

You will need one small bear and one large bear with a tea service in both miniature and doll sizes. Mix together the two tea services. The child must sort out the cutlery and crockery for the right-sized bear.

A similar game can be played using clothing. In this game the child is helped by the fact that the clothes will only fit the right-sized bear. Clothes for a holiday can be packed away in either a large or small suitcase.

☐ Moving day

You will need one large and one small cardboard box with furniture in both miniature and doll sizes. Mix together the pieces of furniture. The child must sort the pieces into the correct box. (Alternatively, you can use a large and small toy van or a large and small doll's house.)

Size and shape sort

Cut out several large circles and several small circles from black card. Provide the child with a large envelope and a small envelope. Ask the child to sort the shapes and place them in the correct envelope.

Instead of circles you can use any big and small shapes. When the child is able to sort one shape by size, ask her to sort out several different shapes. (Remember to keep shapes roughly similar in size, in other words a big circles, a big square and a big rectangle will all be roughly the same size.)

Money for the till

Play shops, using pretend money. Ask the children to sort the money by size into the till. Do they think the bigger the coin the greater its worth?

Size: Big & Small
ACTIVITIES FOR
Home

The following games provide your child with practice at sorting a group of items according to their size.

☐ *Sorting everyday items*

Use household items for sorting games. Remember to choose items that are the same apart from a difference in size. In the kitchen your child can sort cutlery, cups, plates and dishes. In the airing cupboard, socks, vests and pants can be folded into different piles. Likewise, scarves, hats and gloves can be sorted by size. She can also tidy her toys by size, so that big dolls go on one shelf and little dolls go on another; large toy cars go on one shelf and small toy cars go on another.

☐ *Sort and paste*

Cut out several magazine pictures for your child to sort into two piles of big and small. Help your child to stick the pictures in a book. Keep big objects on one page and small objects on another. You could have animals with their young; big and small pictures of the same object (like a teaspoon and a dessert spoon); or pictures of a variety of big and small items (like a thimble, a pin or a button, and an elephant, a house or a tree).

☐ *Sort and post*

Collect together objects in two sizes. You will also need two cardboard boxes or two plastic sweet jars, one large and one small. Show your child how to post an object in each box, then give her the remaining objects. (Make sure these are mixed together.) Encourage her to post the remaining objects. To make the game more interesting, she can pick the objects up with a fish slice, tongs or scoop.

Shoes, shoes and more shoes

Bring out all the family shoes. Ask your child to sort them into different piles according to their size.

Size posters

Help your child cut out pictures of big and small versions of the same item: for example, a big and a little spoon. Ask her to sort them into piles of big and small. Use the pictures to make two posters, one for small items and one for big items.

The following games provide practice in sorting items according to their length. There are ideas for both group and individual work.

☐ *Sort and display by length*

Ask the children to collect objects in different lengths. The children must group objects together that are the same size. They can then be displayed on a table.

☐ *Sort and tidy by length*

Store items by length. Give the children several items to tidy away, such as long ribbons in one box, short ribbons in another.

☐ *Pairs of long and short*

Collect pairs of objects that are identical except for their length. Keep the pairs in a box. Ask the child to sort the objects in two jars: one jar for long, one jar for short.

☐ *Sort a straw*

Cut several straws into two lengths. Provide the child with a long envelope and a short envelope. Ask the child to sort the straws and place them in the matching envelope.

Size: Long & Short
ACTIVITIES FOR
Home

The following games provide your child with practice at sorting a group of items according to their length:

☐ *Sort these out*

Ask your child to sort socks, tights, skirts, ties, scarves and belts by length. You can also use necklaces, bracelets and earrings.

☐ *Pasta sort*

Use some dried spaghetti to make some long and short pieces of pasta. Mix them together and ask your child to sort them into long and short. Afterwards the broken pieces can be used to make some minestrone soup!

☐ *My book of long and short*

Cut out several magazine pictures for your child to sort into long and short. Help your child to stick the pictures in a book. Keep long items on one page, short items on another.

☐ *Laces, ribbons and string*

Collect old shoe laces, ribbons and bits of string. Your child can sort them by length.

☐ *Long and short posters*

Help your child cut out pictures of long and short versions of the same item: for example, a long and a short ruler. Ask her to sort them into piles of long and short. She can paste the long items on a long poster and the short items on a short narrow poster. (Keep the posters quite narrow so as to emphasize the length of the pictures.)

☐ *Sort a straw*

Cut some straws into two lengths. Ask your child to sort the long straws from the short ones. Use the pieces to make necklaces.

These activities can be adapted to work on thick and thin. Look at Section 13, *Visual Resources*, for ideas on suitable materials.

ALTERNATIVE
Materials & Equipment

You may carry out similar activities with a variety of materials that include:

- [ ] everyday objects
- [ ] doll-size items
- [ ] miniature items
- [ ] household items
- [ ] clothes
- [ ] picture material
- [ ] cardboard or plastic templates or stencils

Talk to your child's therapist or teacher about the materials that interest you and your child. Ask them to tick appropriate items from the above list.

Shape
TEACHING ACTIVITY
Sort and Thread

You will need:

several beads in the shape of cubes, several beads in the shape of spheres, two laces for threading

Useful words and phrases:

look, same, different, round, square, necklace, next one

1 Start making a necklace by threading a few spherical beads onto one of the laces.

2 Encourage the child to help you thread the beads.

3 When you have threaded several beads, put the necklace to one side.

4 Start another necklace with the cube-shaped beads. Again encourage the child to thread some beads.

5 When you have threaded several beads, bring out the other necklace and lay both of them in front of the child.

6 Give the child the rest of the beads. Make sure these are mixed together in a box.

7 Ask her to sort the beads into two separate piles, then thread them on the appropriate necklace.

To increase the complexity of the activity

◆ increase the number of shapes;
◆ introduce less familiar shapes;
◆ introduce shapes that are very similar;
◆ ask the child to sort the beads without demonstrating the task first.

Variations

◆ Make bracelets and belts.
◆ Ask the child to put pairs of beads together that have matching shapes.
◆ Ask the child to put the spherical beads in a round box, and the cube-shaped beads in a square box.

The following games provide practice in sorting shapes. There are ideas for both group and individual work:

☐ *Sort a shape*

Give the child several solid geometric shapes to sort. The shapes can be posted into different jars or boxes. To make it more interesting, give the child a fish slice, tongs or scoop to pick up the shapes.

☐ *Display a shape*

Display various items on a table. Ask the children to group the items according to their shape.

☐ *The shape family*

This game is based on the card game, 'Happy Families'. The families are based on shapes, so that there is a Mr and Mrs Square and family, Mr and Mrs Oval, and so on. Draw the family members on cards, incorporating the different shapes into the picture. For example, Mrs Triangle could wear a triangular hat, and the daughter in the circle family could hold a ball. The children must sort the cards into the different families.

Sorting shapes

Cut out three or four shapes from thick black card. Give the child pictures of objects in various shapes. For instance, a balloon, a ball, a cushion and a lollipop might be sorted under a circle, a book, a postcard and a box under a rectangle. (This game can also be played by a group of children. Place the cardboard shapes in the centre of the table and give each child several pictures to sort.)

Make a shape

Make shapes using Plasticine. Try to keep the shapes the same size. Ask the child to sort the shapes into different boxes.

Sort and stick

Cut out a variety of shapes from coloured gummed paper for the children to sort. These can then be used for making pictures of flowers, houses or people.

Shape pictures

Give the children different objects to use as templates for drawings. For example, they can draw around a cup to make a circle, a rubber to make a rectangle and a book to make a square. Ask the children to group the drawings according to their shapes.

Shape
ACTIVITIES FOR
Home

The following games provide your child with practice at sorting a group of items according to their shape:

☐ *Cut and sort the shapes*

Help your child cut out objects from a catalogue. Have ready some envelopes, each marked with a shape. Place one picture in each of these envelopes: for example, a clock in the envelope with a circle, a rug in the one with a rectangle and an egg in the one with an oval shape. Can your child sort the other pictures into the correct envelopes?

☐ *Sort a bead*

Help your child to sort out different-shaped beads. The beads can be stored in the different compartments or drawers of a jewellery box; or use an empty egg box.

☐ *Sort and post a shape*

Collect together objects in two shapes. Mix up the shapes and lay them out on a tray. Use paper shapes that match the objects to label two cardboard boxes or two plastic sweet jars. Start your child off by posting a shape into each of the boxes (jars). To make it more interesting, your child can pick up the objects with a fish slice, tongs or scoop. (Gradually increase the number of shapes your child has to sort.)

☐ *Biscuit box*

Help your child to bake biscuits in various shapes. Once the biscuits have been baked, your child can sort them according to their different shapes. The biscuits can be placed in a plastic mould from an old biscuit tin. These usually have spaces to fit square, round and rectangular biscuits. (Fill any odd-shaped holes with tissue.)

Which suitcase?

Draw several large suitcases, boxes or bags in a variety of shapes: for example, a triangular duffel bag, a square suitcase and a round hat box. Help your child cut out different-shaped items from magazines and catalogues. Mix up the pictures and then ask your child to sort them into the different bags according to their shape.

Sort a shape lotto

Make a shape lotto by cutting out six shapes and sticking them onto a large piece of card. Make six cards that match the shapes. Give your child the cards. Can she match the cards to the lotto cards? To make the game harder, increase the number of matching cards that she has to sort. (Instead of cards, use different-shaped objects to match with the lotto card.)

Shape
ALTERNATIVE
Materials & Equipment

You may carry out similar activities with a variety of equipment that includes the following:

- [ ] three-dimensional solid geometric shapes
- [ ] beads
- [ ] Plasticine, dough or pastry shapes
- [ ] plastic shapes from construction toys

- [ ] cardboard or plastic templates
- [ ] puzzle pieces
- [ ] gummed paper shapes
- [ ] stencils
- [ ] boxes

Talk to your child's therapist or teacher about the materials that interest you and your child. Ask them to tick appropriate items from the above list.

Once children are consistently sorting items by one criterion, they are ready to try sorting by two or three criteria. Here are some ideas:

☐ *Beads*

Ask the child to sort coloured beads for necklaces, bracelets, rings and so on. Give the child beads in different shapes, colours and sizes. Ask her to separate the beads into different boxes. So one box might have large, red, round beads and another box might have small, green, cylindrical beads.

☐ *Shapes from Plasticine*

Make shapes from Plasticine in an assortment of sizes. Ask the children to group shapes together that have both the same shape and the same size. If you use different-coloured Plasticine, the child can sort by colour as well.

☐ *Sticky pictures*

Cut out a variety of shapes from coloured gummed paper. Ask the children to sort them by colour and shape. These can be used for making pictures of flowers, houses or people.

☐ *Sorting envelopes*

Cut out three shapes from black card. Make some large and some small. Mark three large envelopes with a shape that matches the cut-outs. Do the same with three small envelopes. Ask the child to sort the cut-outs into the correct envelope. For example, a large circle will go in the large envelope marked with a circle, and a small rectangle will go in the small envelope marked with a rectangle.

Another variation is to introduce circles in different colours. Ask the child to sort by both size and colour. So a large red circle will go in a large red envelope, and a small blue circle will go in a small blue envelope.

Finally, the child can be given a mixture of coloured shapes in large and small sizes. These can be sorted by colour, shape and size. Try letting the child sort items according to their own criteria.

Many of the sorting activities for colour, size & shape can be adapted to make advanced sorting activities.

P

Visual Sorting
CHECKLIST

Child's name	

Date	Activity	Comments
5/11	My sorting box	Able to sort objects once she has been given a couple of demonstrations (Used the colours red, blue and yellow)

SECTION 7

VISUAL SEQUENCING

Introduction ◆ 111

COLOUR ◆ 112

Teaching Activity 112
Activities for School or Nursery 113
Activities for Home 115
Alternative Materials & Equipment 117

SIZE ◆ 118

Teaching Activity 118
Activities for School or Nursery 119
Activities for Home 121
Alternative Materials & Equipment 122

SHAPE ◆ 123

Teaching Activity 123
Activities for School or Nursery 124
Activities for Home 126
Alternative Materials & Equipment 127

VISUAL SEQUENCING CHECKLIST ◆ 129

S
E
C
T
I
O
N

8

INTRODUCTION

THE ABILITY to recognize and understand the order of visual information presented in a sequence is an important development in the child's perceptual skills. A visual sequence can be either temporal or spatial. A temporal sequence involves the ordering of visual stimuli according to their postition in time. A spatial sequence involves the ordering of visual stimuli according to their position in space. To be able to recognize such sequences requires a number of skills that include matching, recall and anticipation.

This section has visual sequencing activities involving colour, size and shape. It also includes suggestions for using everyday routines to encourage the child's understanding of sequences.

Colour
TEACHING ACTIVITY
Sequence Colour

You will need:

several bricks in equal
numbers of red and yellow

*Useful words
and phrases:*

look, red, yellow,
same, different, first,
next one, train

1 This activity is easier on a flat surface such as a table top.

2 Tell the child you are going to make a train with the bricks. Place a red brick and then a yellow brick on the table. Draw the child's attention to the colour of the brick and the sequence: for example, 'First the red brick, then the yellow brick.'

3 Continue with the sequence until you have several red and yellow combinations.

4 Leave one yellow brick for the child to complete the sequence.

5 Continue the activity but this time leave a red and a yellow brick remaining. Ask the child to complete the sequence using the two bricks.

6 Gradually increase the number of bricks the child has to use to complete the sequence.

To increase the complexity of the activity

◆ gradually increase the number of colours in the sequence;

◆ increase the number of colours to choose from (that is, give the child some coloured bricks that are not in the sequence);

◆ increase the complexity of the colour combination, for example, red, red, yellow;

◆ show the child the sequence and then place it out of sight.

Variations

◆ Use the bricks to build a tower, snake or rocket.

◆ Use beads to make necklaces, bracelets, rings and watches.

◆ Sequence coloured pegs on a washing line.

Always provide several repetitions of the sequence that you want the child to copy. Some children may need to start by adding the last item to a sequence. You can then ask them to complete more and more of the sequence themselves. Start with two colours and gradually introduce more.

☐ Thread a sequence

Use coloured beads, cotton reels or lengths of straw to thread different sequences of colour.

☐ Tidy by sequence

Put blocks of colour on storage boxes and ask the children to put items away following a colour sequence, for example, the red objects first, then the blue and finally the yellow.

☐ Colour croquet

Play colour croquet. You will need several balls and different coloured hoops. (Wrap coloured crepe paper round the hoops.) The children have to hit the ball through the coloured hoops in a specified sequence. Hold up the colour cards to indicate the colour sequence.

☐ Flags

Draw the outline of different flags. Colour in the first flag using a sequence of two or three colours. Ask the child to colour in the remaining flags using the same sequence.

☐ Peg patterns

Make a pattern with pegs in a peg board. Remove one of the pegs. Can the child identify the missing peg from a selection of coloured pegs? Gradually increase the number of pegs you remove. Draw a sequence of coloured dots on a card. Can the child copy the sequence using the pegboard?

☐ Print a sequence

Make print pictures using sequences of colour. Start the child off with one row of shapes printed in different colours. Ask the child to complete the pattern. (Patterns can be made on paper or material.)

☐ Link up a colour

Coloured threading links are available from most educational catalogues. Join the links to form a long chain. Start the child off with a sequence and see if she can continue it. (These links are small, so some children may need supervision when handling them.)

☐ Make a head band

Draw a row of circles on a long strip of card. Colour in the first sequence of colour you want the child to copy. When the child has completed the pattern the card can be made into a head band or bookmark. Children will also enjoy making up patterns for other children to copy.

☐ Make a wall frieze

Make a frieze for the wall: for example, cars in a traffic jam, flowers in a garden, or a giant worm. Show the children a sequence of colours drawn in blocks on a card. Ask the children to copy the sequence onto the wall painting.

Start with two colours and gradually introduce more. At first only ask your child to add the last colour in the sequence. As she becomes more confident you can leave more and more of the sequence for her to complete.

Decorate a fairy cake

Use small coloured sweets or jellybeans to make patterns on fairy cakes. Place two or three of the sweets on one cake. Help your child to copy the pattern onto all the other cakes. (Children will need supervision in this activity to stop any sweets disappearing into mouths or even up noses!)

Candles in a row

Help your child to stick coloured candles in a cake. When your child has correctly completed the sequence she can light the candles and blow them out. (Alternatively, candles can be stuck in a length of Plasticine.)

 Warning: an adult should always be present when matches and candles are being used. Care should be exercised when lighting candles.

Paper chains

Make paper chains using a sequence of colour. Start off the pattern by joining two or three strips of coloured paper. See if your child can choose the colour that comes next.

Straw necklace

Use coloured drinking straws to make beads for necklaces. Cut them into one inch strips. Show your child how to make a pattern. For example, thread a red strip, then thread a blue strip.

Colour a sequence

Draw pictures that use a colour sequence: for example, petals on a flower, plants in a row, sections on a rocket, segments on a snake or caterpillar. Colour in two or three segments, then ask your child to continue the pattern.

S E C T I O N 8

☐ Line up the clips

Attach a row of coloured paper clips to a piece of card. Ask your child to continue the sequence. (Paper clips are small, so your child will need supervision when handling them.)

☐ Sequencing cut-outs

Cut out several circles from different-coloured card or stick gummed paper onto white card. Show your child a pattern. For example, a red circle followed by a yellow circle. Ask her to continue the sequence using the remaining cut-outs.

☐ Peg up a colour

Use coloured clothes pegs to make a pattern. Either use the washing line or put the pegs on a piece of card. Ask your child to continue the sequence using the remaining pegs. Can she make up a sequence by herself?

Colour
ALTERNATIVES
Materials & Equipment

The following items are useful for carrying out sequencing activities:

- ☐ everyday objects
- ☐ household items
- ☐ Duplo, Lego, wooden bricks
- ☐ threading beads

- ☐ links
- ☐ gummed paper shapes
- ☐ plastic shapes

Talk to your child's therapist or teacher about the materials that interest you and your child. Ask them to tick appropriate items from the above list.

Size
TEACHING ACTIVITY
Sequence by Size

You will need:

stacking beakers

Useful words and phrases:

look, next one, too big, too little, beaker, your turn

1 This activity is easier on a flat surface such as a table top.

2 Start with three beakers whose difference in size allows you to slot them together easily. Take the biggest beaker and place the next biggest beaker inside. Give the child the smallest one and encourage her to place it inside the other two.

3 Next, let the child try to slot the three beakers together by herself.

4 Provide feedback on her attempts with verbal and non-verbal cues, such as "No, too big" with a shake of the head; or "Yes, in it goes." But do not use the cues to reprimand the child.

5 Gradually introduce more and more beakers.

To increase the complexity of the activity

◆ gradually increase the number of beakers to be sequenced;
◆ gradually make the size difference between the beakers narrower;
◆ give the child the beakers to sequence without a demonstration;
◆ ask the child to sequence the beakers by placing them in a row.

Variations

◆ Build a tower by standing the beakers upside down.
◆ Ask the child to slot together a Russian doll.

Always provide several repetitions of the sequence that you want the child to copy. Some children may need to start by adding the last item to a sequence. You can then ask them to complete more and more of the sequence by themselves. Start with two size differences and gradually introduce more.

☐ *Store by size*

Store item on shelves in order of size. For example, have three storage jars for storing large, medium and small toy cars.

☐ *Sort and stack*

Ask the child to sort different-sized bricks. These can then be stacked in order of size: for example, a stack of small bricks, a stack of medium-sized bricks and a stack of large bricks.

☐ *Thread a size sequence*

Make necklaces, bracelets and watch straps by threading a sequence of different-sized beads on string: for example, large, medium and small; large, medium and small. Show the children how changing the sequence of beads will create a new necklace.

☐ *Print by size*

Make print pictures using three different-sized blocks. Start the child off by printing one row. Ask the child to complete the pattern. (Patterns can be made on paper or material.)

☐ *Object shapes*

Draw some circles on card using various objects as templates — the bottom of a cup, a coaster, a small side plate, and so on. Cut out the circles and ask the child to arrange the cards in order: small to large and then large to small. Can she match the circles to the original object?

☐ *Size grading puzzles*

Choose puzzles that have pieces graded by size. Remove the pieces and see if the child can still put them in the right sequence.

☐ Line up by size

Ask the children to line up in order of size. Vary the sequence so that sometimes the tallest is at the front of the line and sometimes at the back.

☐ Body prints

Make some prints of hands or feet. Adults can join in too. Discuss the different sizes with the class. Ask them to grade the prints according to size, and then hang the pictures in a row.

☐ Body outlines

Cover one wall in large sheets of white paper. Children have to line up in order of size and stand against the wall. Draw around the outline of each child. When everyone is finished, you can ask the children to find their silhouette. The children can draw in distinguishing features, like glasses and curly hair, once they have found their silhouette.

Start with two sizes and gradually introduce more. At first only ask your child to add the last item in a sequence. As she becomes more confident you can leave more and more of the sequence for her to complete.

☐ *Pots 'n' pans*

Use nesting saucepans, bowls and baking tins to help your child sequence by size. After washing up, encourage your child to stack these items together before putting them away.

☐ *Bake a biscuit*

Your child can use different-sized pastry cutters to make biscuits. When these are baked, they can be arranged in order of size, along with the pastry cutters.

☐ *Measuring spoons*

Ask your child to put these in order of size. Let her use the different spoons in cooking. This will give her an idea of how much food they will hold.

☐ *Family footwear*

If you have shoes in several different sizes, your child can learn how to put them into a sequence. Start with the smallest. She can try each one on to compare it with the size of her foot. (Play this game with different-sized socks or gloves.)

☐ *Everyday objects in sequence*

Collect everyday objects for your child to sequence by size. These might include, coins, stamps, pencils, buttons or boxes.

☐ *Toys in order*

Help your child sequence various toys by size. Toy cars, dolls and teddies can all be ranked by size.

S E C T I O N 8

You may carry out similar activities with a variety of equipment, for example:

☐ everyday objects ☐ threading beads

☐ household items ☐ clothes

☐ Duplo, Lego, wooden bricks ☐ toys

Talk to your child's therapist or teacher about the materials that interest you and your child. Ask them to tick appropriate items from the above list.

Shape
TEACHING ACTIVITY
Sequence Shape

1. Start with two simple shapes: for example, a cube and a sphere. As you thread these onto the cord, draw the child's attention to the sequence, saying, for example, "First the round bead, then the square bead."

2. Continue to thread more shapes with the help of the child.

3. Leave one square bead for the child to complete the sequence.

4. Continue the activity, but this time leave two shapes remaining. Can the child select the two beads that come next in the sequence?

5. If she needs help, encourage her to feel each of the shapes on the cord and compare these with the remaining shapes.

6. Repeat the activity, but this time leave more shapes for the child to sequence.

To increase the complexity of the activity

- gradually increase the number of shapes in the sequence;
- increase the number of shapes to choose from (that is, give the child some shapes that are not in the sequence);
- increase the complexity of the sequence; for example, sphere, sphere, cube;
- show the child the sequence and then place it out of sight.

Variations

- Make necklaces, bracelets, rings and watch straps.
- Ask the child to copy a pattern you have drawn.
- Ask the child to make up a sequence.

You will need:

three-dimensional wooden shapes for threading, threading cord

Useful words and phrases:

look, round, square, thread, next, first

SECTION 8

ACTIVITIES FOR
School or Nursery

Always provide several repetitions of the sequence that you want the child to copy. Some children may need to start by adding the last item to a sequence. You can then ask them to complete more and more of the sequence by themselves. Start with two shapes and gradually introduce more.

☐ *Felt shapes*

Make patterns using felt shapes on a board. Ask the child to continue the pattern.

☐ *Thread a shape sequence*

Make necklaces, bracelets and watch straps by threading a sequence of different-shaped beads on string. (Threading laces and sequencing beads are available from most educational catalogues.) Show the children how changing the sequence of beads will create a new necklace.

☐ *Trace a sequence*

Use different templates to trace a sequence of shapes. Ask the child to continue the sequence using the templates.

☐ *Clown's hat*

Use sequences of shapes as decoration. For example, a column of different shapes can be stuck onto a clown's hat. Ask the children to think up different sequences. Other types of hats can be used in a similar way.

☐ *Body shapes*

Ask the children to form different shapes by lying on the floor. For example, the three sides of a triangle can be represented by three children. Show the children a card with a sequence of shapes. Can they organize themselves to depict the shapes? Are they lying in the correct sequence? Use giant shape cards to help the children to discuss how many children are needed to make the shapes and in what order.

☐ *Print shapes in a sequence*

Make print pictures using sequences of shapes. Use bottle tops, lids from margarine tubs, jars, and so on, to print the shapes.

☐ *Sequencing shape lotto*

Make a sequencing shape lotto. You will need to cut out a variety of shapes from gummed paper. (Remember to use only one colour.) Mark out six squares on a large piece of card. In each square stick a different sequence of shapes. Make six cards that match the squares. Ask the child to match the cards to the lotto board.

Start with two shapes, and gradually introduce more. At first only ask your child to add the last item in a sequence. As she becomes more confident you can leave more and more of the sequence for her to complete.

☐ *Sequencing cut-outs*

Cut out several shapes from stiff white card. Show your child a pattern: for example, a circle followed by a square, and then a triangle. Help your child continue the pattern using the remaining shapes.

☐ *Borders*

Stick gummed shapes onto the edges of paper to make a fancy border for a poem or a picture. At first use shapes in one colour. Later, try introducing shapes in different colours.

☐ *Balloons*

Buy balloons in different shapes, but of the same colour. Help your child decorate the room by putting up groups of balloons. Encourage her to use the same sequence for each set of balloons: for example, a round balloon, followed by a long, sausage-shaped balloon, followed by a long, squiggly balloon.

☐ *Make a sequence*

Use different-shaped pastry cutters to make some shapes from Plasticine. Show your child how to sequence these to make a pattern. Encourage your child to finish off the sequence. Remember to keep all the shapes the same colour.

☐ *Cut and sequence*

Help your child cut out various shaped objects from a catalogue. Draw a sequence of shapes: for example, a circle, a rectangle and an oval. Ask your child to place the shapes in the same sequence. She might have a round clock, a rectangular rug and an oval egg, followed by a round cushion, a rectangular television and an oval balloon.

☐ *Sort and sequence by shape*

Help your child to sort out different shaped beads. Thread the beads on a lace to make a necklace. Can your child follow the sequence you have started?

You may carry out similar activities with a variety of equipment, such as:

- ☐ three-dimensional solid geometric shapes
- ☐ beads
- ☐ Plasticine, dough or pastry shapes
- ☐ plastic shapes from construction toys

- ☐ cardboard or plastic templates
- ☐ puzzle pieces
- ☐ gummed paper shapes
- ☐ stencils
- ☐ boxes

Talk to your child's therapist or teacher about the materials that interest you and your child. Ask them to tick appropriate items from the above list.

127

Sequences in Everyday Life

Encourage the child to notice the natural sequences that occur in her everyday environment. Basic routines such as dressing, eating and sleeping will have a natural order. The adult can increase the child's awareness of the sequence of events in these activities by talking about what is happening, and introducing concepts of first, next, last, and so on.

Children will also enjoy looking at pictures or story books that depict their daily life. This learning can be reinforced for the child by using dolls and miniature items to act out real-life sequences. Older children will enjoy role-play involving imaginary characters and plots.

Here are some everyday sequences:

Everyday activities

- [ ] getting ready for bed
- [ ] having a bath
- [ ] getting dressed or undressed
- [ ] sending a card
- [ ] shopping
- [ ] eating a meal
- [ ] playing a video
- [ ] caring for a pet

Social routines

- [ ] eating at a fast food restaurant
- [ ] getting a book from a library
- [ ] having a swim at the pool
- [ ] going to the park

Special events

- [ ] buying a new pair of shoes
- [ ] having a haircut
- [ ] visiting the doctor or dentist
- [ ] going to a birthday party
- [ ] attending a religious ceremony
- [ ] taking a trip or holiday

Visual Sequencing
CHECKLIST

Child's name	

Date	Activity	Comments
16/5	*Thread a sequence*	*Sequencing three colours in a simple pattern of red, blue and yellow.* *Needs adult to talk her through activity.*

S E C T I O N 8

COMPLEX VISUAL DISCRIMINATION

Introduction ◆ 133

LOOKING FROM DIFFERENT PERSPECTIVES ◆ 135

Activities for School or Nursery   136
Activities for Home   138
Alternative Materials & Equipment   140

LOOKING AT CHANGES ◆ 141

Activities for School or Nursery   142
Activities for Home   143
Alternative Materials & Equipment   144

LOOKING AT ABSTRACT IMAGES ◆ 145

Activities for School or Nursery   146
Activities for Home   147
Alternative Materials & Equipment   149

LOOKING AT DETAIL ◆ 150

Teaching Activity   150
Activities for School or Nursery   151
Activities for Home   153
Alternative Materials & Equipment   154

LOOKING AT DIFFERENCES ◆ 155

Teaching Activity   155
Activities for School or Nursery   157
Activities for Home   159
Alternative Materials & Equipment   161

COMPLEX VISUAL DISCRIMINATION CHECKLIST ◆ 162

SECTION 9

INTRODUCTION

THE ACTIVITIES in this section are designed to challenge children's discriminative abilities. They require the child to deal with complex visual images and abstract representations. They also encourage children to distinguish between items by their differences, as opposed to grouping items by their similarities.

The first three sub-sections help children to recognize objects consistently even when their appearance has altered from the expected one.

1 *Looking from different perspectives:* the way an object appears often depends on the perspective of the viewer. This sub-section encourages the child to explore the effects of distance and angle.

2 *Looking at changes:* this sub-section has suggestions for encouraging the child to notice how growth, ageing or the actual use of an object can change its appearance.

3 *Looking at abstract images:* abstract images such as silhouettes, outline drawings and dot-to-dot pictures are often used to represent objects. The activities in this sub-section help develop the child's ability to recognize items presented in a variety of abstract forms.

The remaining sub-sections encourage the child to refine her discrimination skills so that she can deal with more complex and detailed visual images.

4 *Looking at detail:* children need to develop the ability to distinguish items that are set against a complex visual background. This might involve isolating the detail contained within a composite picture or recognizing an item that is surrounded by other visually similar items. In everyday life this might mean understanding everything in a detailed picture, or being able to find items on a crowded cupboard shelf.

5 *Looking at differences:* visual discrimination involves the child in distinguishing between items that are often visually very similar. These activities help the child to notice small differences between items. Some concentrate on a difference in orientation, where the alignment of an item is different; others involve the substitution or omission of small details. For example, substitution:

omission:

Looking from Different Perspectives

There is no specific teaching activity for this sub-section as discrimination of this sort arises from the child's experience of looking from different viewpoints. It is therefore crucial that the child has the opportunity to have a variety of visual experiences. This is particularly important for children who are less mobile. Use the following:

◆ real objects for the child to explore through touch and vision, before you introduce two-dimensional images;

◆ telescopes, binoculars, microscopes and magnifying glasses to increase the child's awareness of distance;

◆ toys like kites, balloons and mobiles to give the child an opportunity to look close up and then at a distance.

For immobile children:

◆ hang objects and toys on mobiles or elasticated string; twirl them around so the child can see how they look from different angles;

◆ try to vary the child's position so that she views things from a different angle;

◆ make sure the child has the opportunity to see things close up that she normally sees at a distance, and vice versa.

The following activities encourage the child to look at objects and events from different perspectives. The games concentrate on the effects of distance and angle.

What is this?

Take some photographs of common objects from unusual angles. Here are some examples to get you started:

- an upturned bucket (upside down),
- the bottom of a cup (underneath),
- the inside of a hat (inside),
- a pot of flowers as seen from the upstairs window (far),
- a close-up of a light bulb (near),
- an enlarged photograph of a small part of an object, like the holes in a button (enlargement).

Can the children identify the object? Talk about why the objects look different.

Guess the picture quiz

Play a classroom quiz using the above pictures. How many objects can the children identify?

Look out of the window

Ask the children what they can see out of the window. Talk about the way distance changes the perception of size, and how the angle of the viewer can alter the perception of shape. Ask the children to draw a picture of what they can see from the window. They can go outside to make another picture of the same scene from a different angle or distance.

Draw an object

Divide the children into groups. Give each group the same object, but ask them to draw it from different angles: for example, looking down on a flower pot, compared with looking up at it on a shelf. You can also place objects in different positions: for example, upside down, lying down or leaning to one side. Ask the children to compare their drawings.

☐ *Magnify it*

Use a magnifying glass or microscope to look at different objects. Ask the children to draw, first the object and then the magnified image. They can compare the two drawings.

☐ *Look ahead*

Use binoculars and telescopes to look at things in the distance. Talk about what the children can see through the instrument that was invisible to the naked eye.

☐ *Identify the object*

Collect together several similar items and place them in a box. Wrap a duplicate of one of the items in a piece of cloth. Reveal one small part to the child, for example the tip of the spout on a teapot or the bottom of the heel of a shoe. Can the child select its duplicate from the box?

Section 9: Complex Visual Discrimination

S E C T I O N 9

Use the following activities to encourage your child to look at objects and events from different viewpoints:

☐ Walk 'n' look

Go on a 'looking walk'. Encourage your child to look at all the objects and activities around her as she walks along. Places to walk could be as obvious as the local park or as unusual as taking a stroll along the pier at the seaside.

Comment on the way buildings and trees look different viewed from various angles, or how things disappear behind a tree or house then reappear as your view changes.

Point out objects to your child when you are a long way from them. Point out the same ones when you are up close. Talk about how they change: for example, how things increase in size as you get nearer.

☐ Guess my drawing

Start drawing an object from an unusual angle. Can your child guess what it is?

☐ Photo it

Help your child to take photographs of different objects, people and events. Make sure she takes several from different angles. She can also try photographing objects close up and then at a distance. The photos can be mounted on a poster.

☐ High up

Give your child experience of looking at things from a height. This could be from a tall block of flats, a tower, the big wheel at the fair or the cliff top at the seaside.

☐ Sorting far and near

Cut out pictures from magazines of similar objects or people that are taken close up and at a distance. Ask your child to sort the pictures into two groups of far and near.

Peek and guess

The following game can be played at a party. You will need several pieces of stiff card. Cut a circle in each piece, starting with a small hole and then gradually increasing in size. The idea is to cover a picture of an object using the card with the smallest hole. If no one can guess the object, you cover the picture with the card that has the next size hole. You continue until someone guesses the object.

Use the following items to look at the effects of distance:

☐ telescope   ☐ microscope

☐ binoculars   ☐ camera

☐ magnifying glass

Encourage your child to look at the following items from different angles:

☐ everyday objects   ☐ food

☐ household items   ☐ buildings

☐ clothes   ☐ flowers and trees

Talk to your child's therapist or teacher about the materials that interest you and your child. Ask them to tick appropriate items from the above list.

Looking At Changes

Children need to be able to recognize an object despite changes to its appearance. These changes can occur through natural processes like growth and ageing. The way that we use objects can also alter their characteristic outline. For example, an opened umbrella looks very different in size and shape from a closed one. Preparing and cooking food is another process that causes many changes.

There is no specific teaching activity for this sub-section, as each new object or item will be a new learning experience for the child. Experience of watching changes and taking an active role is all part of this learning process. This sub-section has ideas for involving children in exploring these changes and increasing their recognition skills.

S E C T I O N 9

The following activities help children to recognize that an object is the same object even though its appearance has altered in some way.

Match the object to the picture

This activity involves objects whose appearance can easily be changed; for example, a whole orange looks different from one cut into wedges. You will need several pictures of objects as well as the real items themselves. Show the child a picture and then give her an object. Can she make it look the same as the object in the picture? Ideas might include an open box versus a closed box; a whole banana and a peeled one; a flat piece of paper and a crumpled piece of paper; a closed umbrella and an open umbrella.

Picture matching

Collect together two pictures of the same item of food: for example, an uncut loaf of bread and a sandwich; an apple and an apple pie; a bag of potatoes and a bag of chips. Once you have several pairs, you can play a matching game with the children. Talk about how the food has changed, and what actions and cooking methods caused these changes.

Fruit display

Set up a display of different types of fruit. The children can help to cut, chop and slice the fruit to show how its appearance changes. An orange can be peeled, sliced into various shapes, cut into wedges, squeezed, halved or broken down into segments. (A similar activity can be carried out using vegetables.)

Match the pictures

Set out three object pictures in front of the child: for example, a box, an umbrella and an opened deckchair. Show her a picture that is similar but not identical to one of the object pictures, such as a folded deckchair. Can she select the matching object from the three pictures? Gradually increase the number of pictures.

Looking At Changes
ACTIVITIES FOR
Home

Help your child explore the ways in which objects can change their appearance. Here are some suggestions.

☐ *Fruit and veg*

Involve your child in preparing fruit and vegetables. By helping to peel, squeeze and slice, she will learn how they change appearance.

> **⚠ *Warning:* remember to supervise your child carefully if she is using a knife. Choose a soft fruit like a banana for practice in slicing.**

☐ *Watching changes*

Show your child how various items of food change their appearance in the cooking process. Try making popcorn, poppadoms, jam or chocolate sauce.

☐ *Melt down*

Show your child how different foods melt during cooking. Compare this with cold foods that melt when they get warm, like ice-cream, ice-cubes or butter.

☐ *Looking at changes in nature*

Take your child on regular walks during different times of the year. Encourage her to look at the way things change according to the season. Show her the buds of new leaves in the spring, the full-grown leaf in summer and the brown leaf in the autumn.

☐ *Grow a bulb*

Children enjoy having something to grow. Bulbs are a good way of showing your child how things change as they grow.

☐ *Kim's game with a difference*

Place some everyday objects or articles on one tray. Place some duplicates on another tray. Let your child have time to study one tray. Out of her sight, change the appearance of one of the duplicate items. Show her the tray. Can she spot the item that has changed? Ideas include opening a closed fan, opening or closing a box, folding a piece of paper or slicing an orange. You can make the game harder by removing the tray that has the original items, so your child has to do it by memory.

Choose items from the following groups to look at changes in appearance:

- [ ] everyday objects
- [ ] food
- [ ] plants

- [ ] flowers
- [ ] trees

Talk to your child's therapist or teacher about the objects that interest you and your child. Ask them to tick appropriate items from the above list.

Looking At Abstract Images
TEACHING ACTIVITY
Silhouettes

1 Make sure the child has had the opportunity to manipulate the real objects before you introduce the two-dimensional representations.

2 Make several silhouette pictures of the objects, using the coloured sugar paper and white card.

3 Place two silhouette pictures in front of the child. Hand her an object that matches one of the silhouettes.

4 Can she match the object to its silhouette?

5 If necessary, draw her attention to the contour and shape of the object.

6 Encourage the child to talk about what helped her to identify the object.

7 Continue with the remaining objects.

To increase the complexity of the activity

◆ increase the number of silhouettes;
◆ use black silhouettes;
◆ introduce silhouettes using dotted lines;
◆ use objects that are very similar in shape.

Variations

◆ Use ready-prepared materials such as commercially available packs of outline and silhouette nouns.
◆ Use silhouettes of other items like geometric shapes, people, food and so on.

You will need:

stiff white card,
coloured sugar paper,
several everyday objects

Useful words and phrases:

look, silhouette,
names of objects,
same, different

SECTION 9

145

The following activities develop children's ability to identify items presented in a variety of abstract forms:

Pair up the silhouettes

Make a number of playing cards using silhouette pictures. The children can use the cards to play a pairs game. Use pairs of identical pictures or have pictures of related objects like a spoon and cup.

Guess the object

Give the children lots of objects of which to draw outlines on a large sheet of white paper. Make sure the drawings overlap. Can the children guess the objects from the outlines on the paper?

Where's your shadow?

Make a silhouette picture of each child and display it on the wall. Can each child find her silhouette?

Find the shape

Make a pattern by drawing the outline of three-dimensional shapes on paper. Give the child a solid shape to match to one in the pattern.

Find my shadow

Draw the silhouettes of several everyday objects on a lotto board. Ask the child to match the objects to the board. (Alternatively, make several boards with different silhouettes and a group of children can play the game.)

Shadow puppets

Take the children to a shadow puppet theatre, or help them make their own puppets for a class performance.

The following activities will help develop your child's ability to recognize items from their shape or contour.

☐ *Picture jigsaws*

Make some jigsaws from stiff white card. (You can use the white cardboard inserts found in packets of tights or shirts.) Draw the outline of an object such as a teapot or a cup. Cut round the outline so you have a stencil of the object. Repeat this with other object shapes.

When you have several stencils, cut each one in half. Jumble the pieces together. Can your child identify the object from one half of the jigsaw, and then find its matching half? To make it harder, you can cut the shapes into three, four or five pieces. To make the game harder still, use very similar objects: for example, a cup and a beaker, a teapot and a kettle.

☐ *Two-dimensional jigsaws*

Once your child has mastered the above activity, try this game. It is harder for her as she cannot manipulate the pieces. Paste the jigsaw pieces from the above activity onto a piece of paper. Can your child recognize the objects from the jumbled shapes?

S E C T I O N 9

Section 9: Complex Visual Discrimination

☐ *Wrap me a present*

Wrap some distinctively shaped objects in tissue paper. Can your child guess each object?

☐ *Watch the shadow*

Show your child how different hand shapes cast a shadow on the wall. All you need is a torch or angle light. Point the beam at a blank wall in a darkened room. Hold your hands in front of the beam and watch the shadow play.

☐ *Family silhouette*

Make some silhouette pictures of family members. You will need some photographs that give a good side view of the face. Talk to your child about the distinguishing features of different family members.

☐ *Where's my shadow*

Show your child how she casts a shadow on a sunny day. Get her to move around and watch how this changes the shape of her shadow. She can play a game of tag with a difference: instead of trying to touch another child, she must jump on their shadow.

☐ *Draw and match*

Use everyday objects to draw numerous outlines on a giant sheet of paper. These could include a key, a glove, a book, a spoon and so on. See if your child can match the object to its correct silhouette.

☐ *Join up the dots*

Repeat the above activity, but use dotted lines. Once your child has matched the object to an outline, she can join up the dots to see if she is right.

Looking At Abstract Images
ALTERNATIVE
Materials & Equipment

Silhouettes can be made using the following materials:

- ☐ cardboard templates
- ☐ plastic templates
- ☐ coloured sugar paper
- ☐ black sugar paper
- ☐ white card
- ☐ coloured card

Talk to your child's therapist or teacher about the materials that interest you and your child. Ask them to tick appropriate items from the above list.

Looking at Detail
TEACHING ACTIVITY
Matching Shapes to Outlines

You will need:

several solid geometric shapes, a piece of plain white paper, a black felt-tip

Useful words and phrases:

look, names of shapes, trace

1 Let the child examine the solid geometric shapes before you start the activity.

2 Out of sight of the child, draw the outline of one of the geometric shapes. Cover the drawing with a series of diagonal black lines so that the shape is partially obscured.

3 Show the drawing to the child. Can she select the duplicate of the picture from the solid shapes?

4 You may need to help the child by pointing out the distinguishing features of each shape

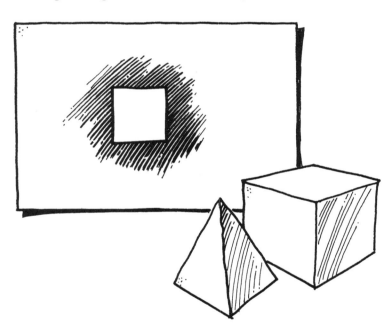

To increase the complexity of the activity

◆ gradually make the lines closer together;

◆ use patterned card or paper instead of plain;

◆ gradually increase the number of shapes the child has to recognize.

Variations

◆ Use horizontal or vertical lines to cover the picture.

◆ Draw everyday objects, clothes, food or vehicles.

◆ Ask the child to trace the outline of the shape, and then copy it onto a different piece of paper.

Looking At Detail

ACTIVITIES FOR
School or Nursery

The following activities will help to develop children's ability to distinguish items that are set against a complex visual background:

☐ Find the animal

You will need a farm play mat and several pairs of miniature animal pieces. Place one set of animal figures on the play mat. Choose one animal from the matching set and show it to the children. Can they find the same animal on the farm? (A similar activity can be played using vehicles on a road play mat.)

☐ Trace and copy

Draw the outline of two shapes on a piece of paper so that they overlap. Ask the child to make a tracing of one shape, and copy it onto a separate piece of paper. Gradually increase the number of overlapping shapes. To make the task harder, use coloured or patterned paper.

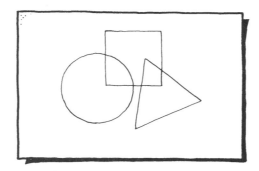

☐ Scribble pictures

Draw some shapes on a piece of paper, then cover the whole paper with scribble using a pencil. Ask the child to colour in all the shapes she can find.

S E C T I O N 9

151

P

Point to the picture

Show the child a composite picture and ask her to point to objects in the picture as you name them.

Free the caged animal

You will need several plastic animal shapes and several matching silhouettes. Cut out a cage with bars from stiff card. Stick the border of the card onto a backing card, leaving one edge unstuck to form a pocket. You should be able to slide the animal silhouettes in and out of the cage. Place four or five plastic animal shapes on the table.

Out of sight of the children slip one of the silhouettes into the cardboard cage. Show it to the children and explain that one of the animals has been caught in the cage. They must help to free it by finding the matching animal from the pieces on the table. When a child has guessed the animal she can release it by pulling the silhouette free of the cage.

Other ideas: fish with different shapes and patterns in a pond obscured by long, wavy fronds; cars in different shapes, sizes and colours hidden in a garage with several windows; different objects or food in a string shopping bag. Make the game harder by placing more than one animal in the cage or having the bars closer together.

Sorting games

Sorting games can be used for looking at detail by changing the background. Place the items to be sorted first on coloured card and then on cards with a pattern. Increase the complexity by choosing a pattern that is very similar to the sorting items: for example, geometric shapes with striped or chequered card. (Alternatively, use coloured and patterned wrapping paper.)

Looking At Detail

ACTIVITIES FOR
Home

The following activities will help your child to notice objects placed against a complex visual background:

☐ *Find the object*

Hide everyday objects, clothing or food amongst other similar items in the room. Try placing a pear in a bowl of fruit, a pen in a pencil case, or a glove in a drawer of gloves and scarves. Show your child an item identical to the one that has been hidden. Can she find its matching pair?

☐ *Spot the object walk*

Take your child for a walk and see if she can spot various objects hidden amongst other similar ones. Ideas might include your child finding a red flower in a multicoloured flower border, or her favourite cereal on a full shelf at the supermarket.

☐ *Hunt the button*

Show the child a button. Can she find the matching one hidden in a box of buttons?

☐ *Can she spot it?*

Show your child a colourful item such as a brightly patterned mug. Ask her to close her eyes, and then hide it somewhere in the room. At first, place it in front of a plain white background: if necessary, you can put a plain white piece of paper or card behind it. Ask your child to find the mug. Next, place the mug in front of something that is very similar in colour or pattern. For example, a red mug could be placed in front of a red cushion, or a mug with a flowery pattern could be placed in front of floral curtains. How long does it take her to find it this time?

☐ *Where's it gone?*

Hide a favourite toy on a crowded shelf of toys or in a jumbled cupboard. Play a game where you see how long it takes your child to find it.

☐ *Picture books*

Look at busy pictures with your child. These are pictures where there is a lot of detail. Ask your child to find different things in the picture.

Section 9: Complex Visual Discrimination

ALTERNATIVE
Materials & Equipment

Use the following materials to create a busy visual background:

- ☐ coloured or patterned card
- ☐ newspaper or magazines
- ☐ coloured or patterned wrapping paper
- ☐ shiny paper

The following games involve the child looking at complex visual images. The more items in an activity, the greater the complexity:

- ☐ doll's house furniture
- ☐ 'pair it' picture games
- ☐ Playmobile
- ☐ books with busy pictures
- ☐ garage with toy cars, buses
- ☐ posters with lots of detail

Talk to your child's therapist or teacher about the materials that interest you and your child. Ask them to tick appropriate items from the above list.

Looking at Differences
TEACHING ACTIVITY
Spot the Mistake

1 Draw a pattern on a piece of card. Start with a simple sequence, for example a cross followed by a circle.

2 Let the child have a turn at drawing the next shape in the sequence.

3 Continue drawing shapes with the child until she is familiar with the pattern.

4 Next, out of sight of the child, draw a square instead of a circle in the pattern.

5 Show the card to the child and ask her to 'spot the mistake'.

6 Draw another sequence out of sight of the child. Put a mistake in the pattern for the child to find.

7 It will be easier if the mistake is near the end at first, but later place it in the middle or near the beginning of the pattern.

To increase the complexity of the activity

◆ gradually increase the number of shapes in the pattern;

◆ use shapes that are very similar.

Variations

◆ Prepare a sequence of simple shapes, but this time omit part of the detail on one of the shapes. For example:

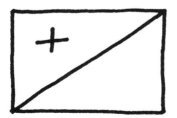 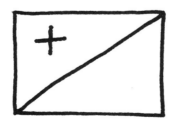 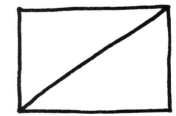

You will need:

some long strips of white card, a black felt-tip

You will need:

Useful words and phrases:

what's different?, same, different, spot the mistake, names of the shapes

S E C T I O N 9

155

2 Prepare a sequence of simple shapes, but this time change the orientation of the shape. For example:

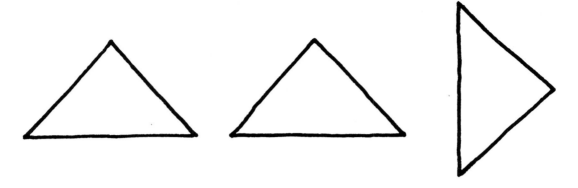

3 Prepare a sequence of simple shapes, but this time change the size of the shape. For example:

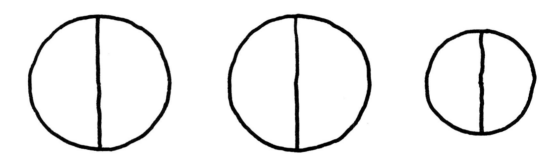

4 Instead of shapes, draw the outlines of everyday objects, toys, food, clothes, and so on.

Looking At Differences
ACTIVITIES FOR
School or Nursery

The following activities encourage children to make comparisons and identify small visual differences between items.

☐ Odd one out

Draw a series of shapes on a chalk board. Make one of them slightly different from the others. Ask one of the children to rub out the odd one and draw in a similar shape to the others.

☐ Fuzzy felt shapes

Stick a sequence of felt shapes on a board, for example, a square, a circle, a square, a circle. Place a different shape within the sequence. Can the child spot the odd one out? Give her a collection of shapes and ask her to replace the odd one with the correct shape.

☐ Draw in the missing part

Draw the outline of three familiar objects on a chalk board. Miss out a small detail from one of the drawings. Ask one of the children to draw in the missing part.

☐ Different-sized objects

You will need two identical items and a third that is identical except in size. Place the three items on the table. Can the children point out which one is different? Introduce items that differ slightly in length, width and height.

☐ Straws or matchstick figures

Construct a series of simple shapes using straws or spent matches. Make one figure so that it is facing in a different direction. Can the children spot the odd figure and correct it.

☐ Build it different

Use building bricks or construction toys to make several identical versions of, say, a building, a wall or a road. Make one slightly different. Can the child rebuild it and make it like the others?

Section 9: Complex Visual Discrimination

☐ Spot the spot

Use a series of coloured spots, for example, red, blue, yellow; red, blue, yellow. Make a mistake in the pattern. Ask the children to spot the mistake. Make this into a game by timing the activity. (Alternatively, use a series of coloured stars or gummed paper shapes.)

☐ Copy the pattern

Draw a pattern on a piece of paper using squares of different colours. Use coloured bricks to copy the pattern, but make a mistake either in the colour sequence or in the shape. Ask the child to correct your arrangement of the bricks so that it matches the paper pattern. You can also use pegs and a peg board to play this game.

☐ Pair it up

Play a pairs game using complete and incomplete pictures. The child has to find the matching pair and then spot the difference before she can keep the cards. (Alternatively, play a game of snap with the cards.) A similar idea is matching pictures that differ in orientation: for example, a pair of chairs where one is facing to the left and the other is facing to the right.

Use the following games to encourage your child to look for small visual differences between items:

☐ *Ornaments*

Use a series of ornaments that are similar in shape, for example three wooden ducks. Turn one round to face a different direction. Can your child spot which one is different? Ask her to make it the same as the others.

☐ *Row of cups*

Put out a row of cups. Change the position of one of the cups. You could turn it upside down or place it so that the handle is facing a different way. Can your child spot the difference? Try this game with other items like saucepans, jars and jugs.

☐ *Draw me a picture*

Draw a series of simple pictures that have one small detail missing: for example, a flower minus one petal, a house with no front door, a face without a nose. Can your child spot what is missing and complete the drawing? Ask your child to draw you a picture with something missing and see if you can guess what it is.

Alternatively, draw some pictures with a deliberate mistake. Draw square wheels on a bicycle, wings on a dog or a cat in a fish bowl! Can your child tell you what is wrong?

☐ *Turn it round*

Use socks, gloves and hats to play this game. Place several in a row, with one facing in a different direction. Ask your child to show you the one that is different and turn it around to match the others.

☐ *Drawing the short straw*

Cut several straws into lengths. Make all the pieces, except one, identical in length. Ask your child to find the one that differs in length.

159

Change the object

Remove some part of an object in the room: for example, the lid from the teapot, the aerial from the television or the lid from the bread bin. Can your child spot what is missing?

I'm different

You and your child can play this game with other family members or with a group of children at a party. First, let everybody study your appearance. Then hide out of sight while you change something about yourself. Try wearing your watch upside down, removing your shoe laces or changing which side you part your hair. How long does it take for someone to spot the mistake?

Spot the difference

Change a familiar display in the room by removing one object. Does your child notice the difference?

Looking At Differences

ALTERNATIVE
Materials & Equipment

The following commercial resources are useful for discrimination activities:

☐ *What's Different?*

☐ *Language in Miniature*

☐ *Multi-Match*

☐ *What's Missing?* (all available from Winslow)

☐ *Visual Variants* (available from Taskmaster)

Talk to your child's therapist or teacher about the materials that interest you and your child. Ask them to tick appropriate items from the above list.

Complex Visual Discrimination
CHECKLIST

Child's name	

Date	Activity	Comments	
3/4	Odd one out	Able to spot a change in size or if something is missing. Not picking up difference in orientation unless prompted by adult.	

P

VISUAL MEMORY & CONCENTRATION

Introduction ◆ 165

BUILDING CONCENTRATION ◆ 166

VISUAL MEMORY ◆ 169

Activities for School or Nursery 171

Activities for Home 174

VISUAL MEMORY CHECKLIST ◆ 177

SECTION 10

INTRODUCTION

THIS SECTION has advice and activities for developing concentration skills and visual memory. All visual perceptual tasks involve memory to a certain extent. The child needs to process, store and retrieve information if she is to recognize and make sense of what she sees. In order for this to take place, she needs to attend long enough to assimilate visual information.

The first part of this section gives guidance on planning activities to develop the child's concentration span. The second part has advice on ways to modify tasks to increase or decrease the memory load for the child in specific activities. Factors affecting the child's ability to remember visual stimuli are also outlined. The final part has a variety of ideas for visual memory activities for school and home.

Building Concentration

In order for concentration skills to develop, the child needs to learn to attend to the dominant stimulus and ignore other extraneous events. At first, this attention is fleeting, as the young infant is attracted to each new visual image. Gradually, the child learns to attend to stimuli for longer and longer periods of time.

At first her attention to activities will be single channelled, and she will need to concentrate on the immediate task. As her attention control matures, she will learn to integrate auditory and visual information, which will allow her to follow oral instructions without having to break off from an activity.

For some children, the ability to maintain concentration for any length of time is difficult, and they require specific help in learning the necessary skills. Below we look at the ways in which the child's concentration skills can be improved.

Guidelines for developing concentration

A child's concentration skills are affected by the nature of the task and the way in which it is presented to her. The following guidelines offer advice on choosing and planning activities. They also include specific strategies to focus and maintain the child's attention to the task.

Use structured activities

A structured activity consists of a sequence of actions that have a definite beginning and end. For example, at the start of a puzzle the pieces are removed; it is completed when all the pieces have been replaced. Try these activities:

- inset trays
- jigsaws
- posting boxes
- stacking toys
- balls on a stick
- slotting games
- nesting beakers
- size-graded abacus
- construction toys

Alternatively, other toys and games can be placed in a box. The act of getting out the toy, and then replacing it in the box at the end of the game, helps to give a structure to the child's play.

Keep activities within the child's abilities

If an activity is too difficult for the child, she will become frustrated. On the other hand, she will become bored by activities that are too simple. Either way, the child will quickly lose interest.

Use familiar activities

Activities should be familiar so that the child is not overwhelmed or frightened by strange toys or new routines. A new toy can be introduced into a familiar routine: for example, nesting beakers can be used instead of bricks to build a tower.

Alternatively, familiar toys can be used in a new routine: for example, show the child how bricks can be used for building trains as well as towers.

Reduce visual and auditory distractions

A quiet, distraction-free environment will help the child concentrate on the activity. (See *Setting up Learning Situations* on page *xi* for more ideas.)

Reduce the number of stimuli

A distractible child will find it easier to concentrate on one toy or item at a time.

Alert the child to the start of an activity

Some children need the adult's help in focusing their attention on the task. At the start of the activity, direct the child's attention to the task by calling her name and talking about the activity. Establish a routine, so that the child is able to follow non-verbal cues that an activity is about to start. For example, by always using a special mat or tray on which to place the activity.

Adjust the length of the activity

You may need to modify the activity to suit the child's attention span, for example marking in a book a place to stop if you know the child is unable to attend to the end. Aim to increase the length of the activity gradually.

Make the activity rewarding

The child is more likely to attend to a task when the reward is intrinsic to the activity: for instance, the thrill of finding the hidden toy inside a set of nesting barrels, or the sense of achievement in building an enormous tower with her toy bricks.

Make your expectations clear to the child

Make sure the child understands what is expected from her in the activity. You may need to help her by demonstrating the task, showing her a model to copy, giving verbal directions and prompting or praising her each time she completes a stage of the activity.

Use task-related language

Talking about the activity will help maintain the child's attention to the task. The child may lose concentration if you start chatting about what she is wearing or the weather outside.

Maintain the child's attention

Some children find it difficult to focus their attention without adult help. Use alerters and prompts during the activity if the child becomes distracted. These can be non-verbal, as when pointing, or verbal, as when giving directions to look.

Use simple instructions

Keep instructions simple and appropriate to the child's language level. Avoid giving a sequence of instructions at the beginning; instead, make them part of the activity.

Reinforce the child's efforts

Offer the child support during the activity. Some children may look to the adult to confirm that they are right before making a choice. Others benefit from feedback on completion of each stage.

Gradually increase the complexity of the task

One way of lengthening the child's concentration span is to increase the complexity of the task. For example, your original activity may have been building a tower with five bricks. Complexity could be increased in a number of ways: by increasing the number of bricks; by showing the child how to extend her play by building a train; or by encouraging her to build more than one tower.

You will find ideas for increasing complexity at the end of all the teaching activities in Sections 4–9.

Use closure clues

These are cues that draw the child's attention to the end of an activity: for example, "All gone", "Finished". They help the child understand that the activity has been completed, and also include non-verbal cues like putting the game away in a box or clapping her success. A change in intonation will also help to signal to the child that she has completed the task appropriately.

Acknowledge the child's efforts and success

Praise the child and reinforce her efforts. For example, naming the pieces in a puzzle she has just completed will give her a sense of achievement.

When observing a child's response to activities, you need to note the following:

◆ Did she show interest in the activity?

◆ Was the activity initiated by the child or the adult?

◆ How long did she attend to the activity?

◆ Did she frequently leave the activity and then return to it?

◆ What prompts were used to maintain her attention to the task?

◆ Did she tolerate the adult's participation in the activity?

◆ How did the adult participate?

◆ Did she need adult help to complete the activity? If so, what prompts were used?

Visual Memory

All visual perceptual tasks involve memory to a certain extent. Activities can be modified to increase or decrease the memory load for the child.

The child's ability to remember visual stimuli will be affected by the factors listed below, some of which relate to the child and others to the nature of the task presented to the child:

The child's visual skills: a child with a visual impairment may take longer to discriminate and therefore process visual information. Check whether the child wears glasses and that they are clean. Seek the advice of professionals such as a teacher for the sensory impaired.

A busy visual environment: the child will be distracted and find it hard to attend with competing visual stimuli.

A noisy background: the child will be distracted and find it harder to attend with competing auditory stimuli.

The child's health and well-being: a child who is tired, unwell, or otherwise not comfortable, will find it difficult to attend.

The child's language level: a lack of language skills may make extra demands on the child's ability to complete an activity, thus affecting her memory capacity.

The child's familiarity with the adult: the child may become withdrawn or 'play up' when with an unfamiliar adult.

A formal situation versus an informal situation: it may be harder for the child to remember under the pressure of a test situation. On the other hand, the child may be too relaxed in an informal atmosphere and be less inclined to attend.

Time pressures: is there a time limit on the activity? Is it near dinner time? Is the child competing with another child? All these pressures may have an adverse effect on the child's ability to remember.

The age of the child: memory skills are linked to language and develop with age.

The cognitive abilities of the child: memory skills are linked to the cognitive level of the child.

Activities can be modified to alter the memory loading for the child. Below is a list of factors that can increase the demand on the child's memory skills:

◆ new activities;

◆ unfamiliar materials;

◆ time limit on the completion of the task;

◆ the amount of language the child is required to understand during the activity;

◆ a task involving several skills rather than one skill;

◆ visual stimuli that are very similar;

◆ the complexity of the visual stimuli;

◆ a delay before the child can respond;

◆ the level of visual skill: for example, visual matching is easier than visual sorting;

◆ the number of visual stimuli the child has to choose between;

◆ the number of items the child has to remember;

◆ asking the child to recall a sequence;

◆ introducing a distraction before the child is allowed to recall items;

◆ the length of an activity.

When planning activities to develop memory, look at the suggestions for increasing the complexity of the activities in Sections 4–9 of this manual.

The following activities encourage children to remember visual information, and to be more visually alert in everyday situations:

That's my sign

Assign to each child a picture or symbol. Stick the sign on the child's coat peg, tray, chair and other personal possessions. The child has to remember the picture to find her coat or seat. Change the signs regularly. The signs can be linked to topic work on matching and discrimination.

Remember your neighbour

Let the children take it in turns to close their eyes and remember the colour of a neighbouring child's jumper. This could be a child seated behind, next to or in front of them. This way the child has several colours to remember. Can the child close her eyes and remember the colour of her own jumper? Vary the activity by asking about the colour and length of hair, types of clothing and whether shoes have buckles or laces.

Find the matching colour

Show the children a card with a single block of colour. Place it out of sight. How many things in the room can they point to that have the same colour? Make the task harder by using different shades — dark red and light blue, for instance.

Remember what you see

First thing in the morning, ask the children to say what they saw on the way to nursery or school.

What's changed?

While the children are not looking (perhaps over lunch time), remove an item from a familiar display. Can the children spot what is missing? Alternatively, you could add an object or swap the position of two items.

Touch the object

Choose one child to go and touch an object or toy in the room and then return to the group. Another child is chosen to go and touch the same item and then one other. Gradually build up the number of items the children have to remember.

Who's missing?

Select one child from the group and ask her to close her eyes. Point to another child to leave the room. The first child opens her eyes and tells who has left the room. The rest of the group can change places to make it harder for the child to remember.

Posing pairs

Two children are chosen from the group and placed in a pose. This could be standing back to back or one sitting and one standing, and so on. One child from the watching group is asked to close her eyes. The posing pair change position. The child opens her eyes and then has to rearrange the couple into the previous position. Gradually increase the number of children and make the changes more subtle.

Find the object

Show the child a picture of an object. Hide the picture and ask the child to point to the matching object in a composite picture.

Picture menu

Set up a pretend restaurant using toy food. Make a menu card using pictures of the toy food. The customers make their choice of food by pointing to a picture. The waiter has to remember the pictures in order to bring the correct meal.

Remember the sequence

You will need a set of stacking beakers for this activity. Tell the child that you are going to make a staircase. Place the beakers upside down in a row, starting with the smallest and building up in size to make the steps. Draw the child's attention to the sequence, and then ask her to close her eyes. Remove one of the beakers and move the others together so that there is no space. Ask her to point to the place from which the beaker was removed. Give her the beaker to slot into place if she is unable to guess.

Remember the picture

You will need several duplicate pairs of object pictures. Place three pictures in front of the child. Next show her a picture that matches one of the three. Give the child time to study the picture, then lay it face down on the table. Can the child point to the picture that matches the hidden one? It may be necessary to let the child match the pictures at first, until she has got the idea. Gradually increase the number of pictures. This game can also be played with objects.

Copy my actions

Play obstacle races where the children have to remember a sequence of actions you have shown them: for example, jump over a box, skip to a chair.

Crocodile's breakfast

You will need a crocodile puppet. (Alternatively, use another animal puppet that has a large mouth.) Place several coloured bricks on the table. One child closes her eyes. Another child is given the crocodile puppet, who promptly eats one of the bricks. The child opens her eyes and has to guess the colour of the brick that has been eaten. (Objects and pictures can be used in a similar way.)

These games will help your child's visual memory. Many of the activities can be played as party games.

☐ *What's missing?*

Place five everyday objects on a tray. Let your child have a few minutes to memorize the items, and then cover them with a large cloth. Surreptitiously, remove one of the items and hide it. Take off the cloth. Can she tell you which object is missing? (It is important that your child has some way of identifying the objects. The use of an appropriate gesture or sign is an acceptable alternative to naming the objects. So, if a cup was the object removed, a gesture that indicates drinking would be sufficient.)

☐ *What's new?*

Try the above activity, but this time add an object. Can your child spot which object is new?

☐ *Snapshot*

Allow your child a few minutes to study your appearance. (The idea is for her to take a 'mental snapshot'.) Remind her to look at your clothes, your hairstyle, make-up and jewellery. Ask her to close her eyes, and then change something about yourself. Try removing a piece of clothing or untying a scarf or tie. Gradually increase the number of changes, and make them more subtle, such as changing the side you part your hair or putting your watch on the other wrist. This is also an enjoyable game to play at parties.

What's changed?

Help your child arrange four or five items of miniature furniture in a doll's house, garage or shop. Ask her to close her eyes and then change the position of one of the pieces. Can the child replace the object in the correct position? Instead of removing an item, add one. Can she spot the difference? Introduce some small dolls. They can change position between sitting, standing and lying. They can also be next to, behind, under and so on. At first, start with one room, then gradually increase the number of rooms you use, and the number of changes to the arrangement.

Follow my movements

Teach your child a set of movements and then combine them into a dance routine! See if your child can think up her own actions. Movements can be as simple as a hop, a skip or stretching arms above the head.

Three pictures in a row

Cut out three pictures of objects from a magazine. Place them in a row in front of your child. After she has looked at them carefully, turn over the pictures. Can your child recall what she has seen? Can she remember the correct order in which the pictures were placed? (You can also use pictures of people carrying out various actions like jumping and running.)

Laying the table

Let your child lay the table for lunch. Can she remember the correct settings? Make it harder by adding glasses, napkins and condiments.

Pass the action

Play this party game. One person starts with an action, for example clapping her hands twice. The next person claps twice, then the next, and so on until the clapping has 'passed' round the circle. When everybody has got the idea, another action can be added, for example rubbing your nose. The idea is for each person to remember all the actions and to do them in the correct order. Otherwise she is out of the game.

Action songs

Sing action songs where your child has to put into sequence several actions; for example, *Ring-a-ring of Roses*, has a definite sequence and helps build up anticipation.

Pairs game

You will need several pairs of object picture cards. (These are available from toy shops.) Start with a small number of pairs, perhaps four or five. Show the child that each picture has a matching pair, then place them face down on a table or the floor. Select the first pair of cards. Use simple language to make it clear to your child whether your cards match or not: for example, "No, different" or "Yes, same". Help your child's memory skills by naming the pictures and drawing attention to where the cards are placed. Let your child have the next turn. The winner is the player who has found the most matching pairs.

Snap pairs

Increase the excitement by combining the previous game with 'Snap'. When two matching cards are turned over, the winner is the first player to shout, "Snap!"

Colouring

Can your child colour pictures from memory? Try pictures of fruit, animals or flowers. This is a good follow-up activity to the park, zoo or farm.

Reading

Start developing your child's reading skills by encouraging her to recognize the first letter of her name. Point out the letter on food packages, in shops, or on books at home.

Shopping list

Go shopping with a visual shopping list. Show your child a picture of the item you want. Can she find it in the supermarket?

Clothes in a suitcase

Ask your child to help you place some clothes and toiletries in a suitcase. Ask her to close her eyes, and then change the position of two items. Can she spot the difference in position?

Visual Memory
CHECKLIST

Child's name

Date	Activity	Comments
16/12	Pass the action	Remembered four actions but confused the order

HOLIDAY PROJECTS

Introduction ◆ 181

HOLIDAY VISUAL SKILLS PROJECTS ◆ 182

HOLIDAY PROJECTS CHECKLIST ◆ 185

SECTION 11

INTRODUCTION

THIS SECTION has numerous suggestions for reinforcing the child's perceptual skills and expanding her visual experiences. Activities range from special outings to more everyday experiences such as attending a playgroup. These activities are aimed at parents, carers or others in close contact with the child who may want to continue working on the child's visual skills during school holidays or a break from therapy. Some ideas may be new, while others may reassure users that the activities in which the child already participates will encourage her visual skills. There should be an activity to suit everyone, regardless of financial or social needs. Some are for whole family participation and others are for the child alone.

Holiday Visual Skills Projects

Below are some ideas for helping your child's visual skills during the holidays. They include places to visit, special events and ideas on how you can join in the fun. Check your local paper for dates of special activities or details of places to visit. There is often lots of information at your local library about coming events. Look out for free entry or special rates for children.

☐ Mime show

Mime focuses attention on the visual aspects of our behaviour. Children love to watch this unusual form of entertainment. Look out for mime artists at carnivals, fun days and other public events.

☐ Clowns

Clowning is a comic form of mime, which children all over the world love to watch. Your child can watch clowns at the circus. There are also more and more opportunities for children to participate in clowning workshops. Check your local library for information.

☐ Kites

Kites attract the attention of both adults and children. Their quick, darting movements encourage children's visual tracking skills. You do not have to own a kite. You can always go and watch other people's.

☐ Firework displays

Take your child to an organized firework display. She will be able to see a wonderful array of patterns and colours. If she is old enough, let her hold a sparkler. She can wave it around to make different patterns.

☐ Special exhibitions at museums

Many museums now have areas designed specifically for children. Displays are placed at an appropriate height, and interaction is encouraged. They stimulate all the senses, including sight. Look out for special exhibitions during the holidays.

Parades or carnivals

Watch and marvel at the colourful floats that are the essence of any procession. Many carnivals take place in the summer, but there are also marching bands and other parades during the rest of the year.

Art exhibitions

Libraries and community centres often have exhibitions of work by local artists. Encourage your child to look at the display. Find out what she likes and why she likes it.

Special days

Many local councils, community centres, hospitals, schools and day nurseries organize or take part in special event days for users of their services. Activities range from fun days to sports competitions. Whatever the theme, it is guaranteed to stimulate all the senses.

Funfairs

Children of all ages love funfairs. There are many sights, sounds and smells to excite your child before she even takes her first ride. Look out for mini-funfairs set up at festive times of the year.

Historical sound and light shows

These types of show are becoming increasingly popular. They consist of reconstructions of scenes from the past, using lifelike models with special effects from sound and light. This way your child can see, hear, feel and smell the past. Some famous ones in the United Kingdom include Canterbury Tales at Canterbury and the Vikings at York. As these can be expensive, you might like to save this activity for a treat.

Holidays

If your are on holiday or visiting your family in another country, your child will experience many new and different sights. You do not have to go abroad to give your child new experiences. A different town, a new house or even a different routine can stimulate your child to look around her.

Scrapbook

Help your child choose her best drawings and paintings to make into a scrapbook or collage.

Playgroups

Playgroups provide opportunities for the sort of messy activities that are not possible at home. Children can learn about colour and shape through painting, modelling and making collages.

Look and find

When you are out walking, encourage your child to look for examples of one particular object. These might be door knockers or stickers in car windows. Talk about the differences and similarities between the different types of object. Other ideas include finding as many things as possible in a certain colour or counting all the animals and birds you see. Look out for very small or inconspicuous objects, as well as larger ones.

Collection

Collect items on your walk. At the seaside you will find shells, pebbles and small stones; in the countryside you can collect fallen leaves, twigs and grasses. Help your child look at different shapes, colours and patterns. She can draw a picture, trace over or around an object, or make a special display with the pebbles she has collected.

Flower shows

Flowers are lovely to look at, and they also have many different scents to stimulate the sense of smell. There are also gardens designed for partially sighted and the blind, where flowers and plants are suitable for tactile exploration.

Grow an egg head

There is nothing like a living thing to encourage children to look. Help your child to grow an egg head. You will need some eggs, egg cups, felt-tips, some mustard and cress seeds, and cotton wool.

Place your egg in an egg cup, and remove the top part of the shell. You need to make a small hole about 2.5 cm wide. Carefully empty the contents into a bowl. (Use them to make scrambled eggs!) Gently wash out the inside of the shell with soapy water and wait for it to dry. Your child can draw a funny face on the shell with coloured felt-tips.

Fill the egg shell with cotton wool, and moisten it with a little water. It should come up to about 1.5 cm from the top. Sprinkle a thick layer of seeds onto the cotton wool. Place the egg away from draughts, in a sunny position. The seeds should start growing in about a week. The sprouting seeds have the appearance of tufts of green hair. Like other plants, your egg heads will need regular watering.

Holiday Projects
CHECKLIST

Child's name	

Date	Activity	Comments
16/5	Collection	Visit to the seaside: collected shells and pebbles from the beach. Very interested in the different patterns

SECTION 11

VISUAL SKILLS IN THE SCHOOL CURRICULUM

Introduction ◆ 189

TOPICS ◆ 190

What is sight?	190
Why is sight important?	190
Colour	191
Shape	191
Visual arts	192
Clothes	192
Design	193
Mime	193

INTRODUCTION

VISUAL PERCEPTUAL skills are important to many areas of life and learning. The school curriculum can both reinforce and develop these skills. It can also encourage children to be more visually aware of their surroundings, and to use sight as another channel for exploration.

This section provides suggestions for various topic-based activities for use in the classroom. They are aimed at older, more able children, who have some expressive language skills and can take some part in discussions. They provide opportunities for the children to work co-operatively as partners, in small groups or as a whole class. The use of a variety of communication styles is encouraged.

Visual Skills in the School Curriculum
TOPICS

The following topics can be used to help develop the children's perceptual skills as well as supporting the curriculum in key subject areas.

What is sight?

Children can:

- [ ] find out about the eye and how we see;

- [ ] discuss the uses of sight: to read; for safety (crossing the road, for instance); to enjoy, as in visual entertainment like television and the arts;

- [ ] discover how eyesight is measured;

- [ ] experiment with different inventions that change the way we see things, such as three-dimensional glasses, tinted lenses and instruments like 'bugeye' which multiply images.

Why is sight important?

Children can:

- [ ] make a list of reasons why sight is important to them;

- [ ] experience being blind by wearing a blindfold, and describe what it feels like not being able to see;

  Warning: **if you are helping children to experience being blind, make sure you supervise them well. They should always be escorted if they go outside the classroom. Make sure the area is safe and you have removed any dangerous obstacles for this activity.**

- [ ] discuss the causes of blindness and find out about aids for the blind;

- [ ] explore different ways of enhancing vision, such as binoculars, glasses, a microscope or a magnifying lens;

- [ ] learn the deaf–blind manual alphabet (have a finger spelling competition, where the children have to learn to spell a certain number of words);

- [ ] experiment with using different senses to compensate for loss of sight, such as touch, smell and hearing;

- [ ] do a project on Braille.

Colour

Children can:
- [ ] find out about colours by mixing different paints;

- [ ] discuss how different colours make them feel;

- [ ] look at the way colour was used by the great painters;

- [ ] make a list of the different events, feelings and beliefs that are represented by colour: for example, red might mean stop, or be representative of a political party;

- [ ] record the different colours they see in their environment;

- [ ] carry out a project on the use of colour in advertising;

- [ ] study the use of colour in clothing: for instance, how colours are chosen for uniforms, how dyes are produced;

- [ ] paint a colour wheel to illustrate the colour spectrum;

- [ ] discuss why colour is important in food;

- [ ] describe the way colour is used by animals to camouflage or to attract a mate.

Shape

Children can:
- [ ] explore the shape of different objects. Are they smooth? Do they have pointed or straight edges? Do they roll? Do they stand up?

- [ ] look at shapes in the environment: for example, the spiral shape can be found in cloud formations, shells, water emptying down a plug hole, screws and springs;

- [ ] explore natural versus man-made shapes: stones, shells, leaves versus nuts, screws, boxes;

- [ ] compare geometric shapes with real-life shapes, for example a square with a window;

- [ ] discover how shapes have changed in architecture, and what influenced these changes.

SECTION 12

Visual arts

Children can:

- ☐ discuss the development of different art forms through history;

- ☐ compare art from different countries;

- ☐ visit a local art gallery, sculpture garden or craft exhibition;

- ☐ enter their work in an art competition (or hold their own and invite a special guest to pick a winner);

- ☐ express an idea using different mediums such as pictures, music or dance, and then compare the results;

- ☐ look at the importance of art to different religions and in different cultures.

Clothes

Children can:

- ☐ discuss why we need clothes;

- ☐ have a competition to design a school uniform;

- ☐ talk about the shapes and colours of clothes;

- ☐ make a costume for a fashion parade;

- ☐ look at the different shapes used in dressmaking paper patterns, and see how these are made up into different garments;

- ☐ draw the different costumes worn by people through the ages;

- ☐ find out about the clothing sizes of the children and adults at school (the results can be recorded on a table or graph);

- ☐ use computer graphics to design an outfit;

- ☐ discover the national costumes of the world;

- ☐ visit a museum to find out how clothing has changed through history, and to learn about the inventions which accompanied these changes (such as a loom, a crinoline frame or a trouser press);

- ☐ visit a clothing or weaving factory;

- ☐ base a project on wool or another well-known fabric or material;

- ☐ hold a debate on whether school children should wear a uniform.

Design

Children can:

- [ ] discuss the skills required in design, such as spatial awareness, creativity and technical skills;

- [ ] design a futuristic house: they must provide a ground plan as well as ideas on materials;

- [ ] visit a variety of buildings and compare their design;

- [ ] talk about the link between the design of an object and the need for safety, attractiveness, ergonomics and so on;

- [ ] have a competition to design a kite;

- [ ] write out the instructions for making their kite, and use photographs or pictures to illustrate the design stages;

- [ ] try to reproduce a design from memory: the design could be a construction of wooden bricks, straws, plastic cups or any other suitable material;

- [ ] visit a design studio to see the creation of a product.

Mime

Children can:

- [ ] discuss the meaning of 'mime';

- [ ] discover the use of mime in the theatre;

- [ ] see a mime show;

- [ ] experiment with miming everyday actions;

- [ ] discuss the use of gesture in different situations, for instance directing the movement of planes on the tarmac or as a secret code;

- [ ] explore the use of mime as a form of entertainment by comparing silent movies with Japanese theatre, and so on;

- [ ] discuss how gestures are used with spoken language, and what these gestures mean;

- [ ] discuss how the meaning of gestures varies between different cultures.

VISUAL RESOURCES

Introduction ◆ 197

LOOKING BOX   ◆ 198

MAKE A MOBILE   ◆ 199

VISUAL RESOURCES LIST   ◆ 201

SECTION 13

INTRODUCTION

This section provides a comprehensive list of toys, materials, equipment and everyday items for use in attention and visual perceptual activities. It also gives directions for making mobiles, and suggestions for items to collect for a visual skills resources box.

The following information can be used by parents, carers and teachers to stimulate ideas for adapting and extending activities and games. Using a variety of equipment will help the child to generalize her skills. This section can also be used to identify appropriate items for a specific child.

Looking Box

Make your own visual skills resource box. The following objects can be collected and kept together in a large box.

- [ ] laser discs
- [ ] holograms
- [ ] glove, finger or pop-up puppets
- [ ] kaleidoscope
- [ ] yo-yo
- [ ] cardboard tubes (long and short)
- [ ] coloured, 3-D or fun glasses
- [ ] assorted solid shapes
- [ ] seashells
- [ ] pebbles
- [ ] assorted textured and coloured paper
- [ ] reflective paper
- [ ] assorted textured and coloured material
- [ ] magnifying glass
- [ ] mirror
- [ ] torches
- [ ] fans

- [ ] balloons
- [ ] feathers
- [ ] bubbles
- [ ] Christmas decorations
- [ ] coloured cellophane
- [ ] hand-held windmills
- [ ] wind-up toys
- [ ] flags or streamers
- [ ] ribbons
- [ ] face masks, fancy dress or masquerade eye-masks
- [ ] silver and gold paper cake cases
- [ ] face paints, false eyelashes or moustache
- [ ] spinning tops
- [ ] fun wigs
- [ ] party blowers

Looking Box

Make a Mobile

Make your own mobile using household items. Coat hangers provide an ideal frame, and come with a ready made hook. Alternatively, use a length of cane or the frame from an old lamp shade. Use something strong to hang the frame, such as the wire used for hanging pictures or nylon fishing line.

Remember these safety rules:

◆ make sure the frame is securely attached;

◆ do not overload the frame; it will fall down if it is too heavy;

◆ attach items securely;

◆ do not place the mobile above or next to any heat source;

◆ hang it above head level.

The following items can be hung on the mobile:

- ☐ Christmas decorations
- ☐ cardboard shapes covered in coloured, shiny or textured paper
- ☐ transparent materials like cellophane or net curtain
- ☐ odd household items like cotton reels or scouring pads
- ☐ pompoms
- ☐ feathers
- ☐ colourful figures cut from magazines
- ☐ brightly coloured buttons, beads

- ☐ keys in assorted shapes and sizes
- ☐ squeaky toys
- ☐ little bells
- ☐ crumpled paper
- ☐ horse chestnuts, acorns or leaves
- ☐ silver, gold or metallic wrapping paper
- ☐ streamers
- ☐ different coloured ribbons, wool or string
- ☐ sequins, beads and other glitter sewn or glued onto strips of material or paper

S E C T I O N **13**

Alternatives to mobiles include the following:

- [ ] wind chimes
- [ ] cardboard figures hung on thick elastic
- [ ] tin foil milk bottle tops strung on string
- [ ] everyday objects hung on string or thick elastic
- [ ] balloons tied to a piece of thick elastic (Vary the shapes and colours. Make them more interesting by covering them with glitter or sticking paper streamers on them.)

Mobiles are very versatile. Make the most of them by using the following tips:

- vary the materials or objects for the mobiles;
- choose items that make a noise, as well as being visually interesting;
- hang the mobile in different locations (avoid very sunny windows where the glare would make it difficult to see);
- group mobiles together;
- frames suitable for suspending toys are available from special needs educational catalogues. These can be used for children who are in a prone position. Frames allow the child to explore by touch as well as by looking. Make sure that items are firmly attached and are robust enough to be handled;
- place yourself behind the mobile: this way the child can see you and the mobile.

VISUAL RESOURCES
List

The following is a list of toys, equipment and everyday materials for use in visual attention and perceptual activities.

Objects and toys that have movement

- [ ] wind-up toys
- [ ] spinning tops
- [ ] toy carousel
- [ ] rocking toys
- [ ] sound-activated toys
- [ ] pull-along toys
- [ ] balls
- [ ] transparent balls containing a spinning figure
- [ ] marbles
- [ ] mobiles
- [ ] wind chimes
- [ ] yo-yos
- [ ] toys hung on a piece of elastic or long spring
- [ ] push-and-bounce-back toys
- [ ] Newton's cradle
- [ ] giant egg timer
- [ ] kites

Toys and equipment for looking at light

- [ ] magic lanterns
- [ ] torches
- [ ] candles
- [ ] toys and books which have flashing lights
- [ ] bubble tubes
- [ ] lullaby light shows
- [ ] fairy lights

Toys and equipment for looking at colour

- [ ] kaleidoscope
- [ ] paints or crayons
- [ ] bricks
- [ ] threading beads
- [ ] counters
- [ ] picture books
- [ ] coloured streamers
- [ ] coloured gummed paper
- [ ] computer graphic programmes

Toys that develop awareness of size

- [ ] nesting boxes
- [ ] Russian dolls or eggs
- [ ] stacking toys
- [ ] graded rings on a stick
- [ ] puzzles
- [ ] size-graded puzzles
- [ ] posting boxes
- [ ] different-sized buckets and trays for sand and water play
- [ ] dolls or figures with clothes

Toys that develop awareness of shape

- [ ] posting boxes
- [ ] shape form boards
- [ ] floor jigsaws or mosaics
- [ ] different-shaped buckets and trays for sand and water play
- [ ] pastry shape cutters
- [ ] templates or stencils
- [ ] different-shaped bricks
- [ ] beads

Items for matching and sorting by colour

- [ ] beads
- [ ] buttons
- [ ] bricks
- [ ] counters
- [ ] crayons or pencils
- [ ] laces
- [ ] pegs
- [ ] material
- [ ] paper
- [ ] plastic plates, cups or cutlery
- [ ] mats
- [ ] hoops
- [ ] balls
- [ ] sweets
- [ ] cotton reels
- [ ] wool
- [ ] balloons
- [ ] boxes
- [ ] paper clips
- [ ] gummed paper and paper shapes
- [ ] plastic carton tops
- [ ] plastic shapes from construction toys
- [ ] straws
- [ ] cars
- [ ] Plasticine
- [ ] paints

Items for matching or sorting by size (big/small)

- [ ] side plate/dinner plate
- [ ] miniature cup/real cup
- [ ] real cup/breakfast cup
- [ ] small toy brick/large toy brick
- [ ] A5 paper/A4 paper
- [ ] small shirt button/large coat button
- [ ] miniature book/large picture book
- [ ] pingpong ball/tennis ball
- [ ] tennis ball/football
- [ ] small square piece of wood/large square piece of wood
- [ ] small pill or button box/large shoe box
- [ ] single portion box of cereal/family pack of cereal
- [ ] miniature objects/real-size objects
- [ ] small safety pin/large safety pin
- [ ] small paper clip/giant paper clip
- [ ] small doll furniture and accessories/large doll furniture and accessories

- [ ] hand towel/bath towel
- [ ] travel-size soap/bath-size soap
- [ ] travel-size toothpaste/regular-size toothpaste
- [ ] travel shampoo bottle/family shampoo bottle
- [ ] travel alarm clock/bedside alarm clock
- [ ] small sand bucket/large sand bucket
- [ ] different-sized containers: bowls, plastic lunch boxes, tin foil trays
- [ ] doll's clothes/children's clothes
- [ ] miniature picture/large framed picture
- [ ] child's toothbrush/adult toothbrush
- [ ] small stones or pebbles/large stones or pebbles
- [ ] pocket comb/regular-size comb

SECTION 13

Items for matching or sorting by size (long/short)

- [ ] string or wool
- [ ] pencils, pens or crayons
- [ ] pieces of chalk
- [ ] strips of paper
- [ ] toy trains
- [ ] toy cars or buses
- [ ] straws
- [ ] lollipop sticks
- [ ] pieces of wood
- [ ] pipe cleaners
- [ ] strips of raffia
- [ ] scarves
- [ ] ribbons
- [ ] socks
- [ ] belts
- [ ] ties
- [ ] feathers
- [ ] necklaces and bracelets
- [ ] shoe laces
- [ ] grass or twigs
- [ ] rulers
- [ ] candles

Items for matching or sorting by size (thick/thin)

- [ ] books
- [ ] blocks of wood
- [ ] sheaves of paper
- [ ] lines drawn on paper
- [ ] slices of bread
- [ ] pieces of material
- [ ] strips of linoleum
- [ ] strips of carpet

Choose similar items that only differ in width, not length, size and so on.

Items for matching or sorting by shape

- [ ] solid geometric shapes
- [ ] boxes
- [ ] beads
- [ ] buttons
- [ ] balloons
- [ ] dough shapes
- [ ] Plasticine shapes
- [ ] pastry shapes
- [ ] plastic shapes from construction sets
- [ ] plastic or cardboard templates
- [ ] puzzle pieces
- [ ] gummed paper shapes
- [ ] cardboard or paper cut-outs
- [ ] stencils

Sorting trays

☐ tin foil dishes

☐ paper cups

☐ plastic plates

☐ wicker baskets

☐ boxes

☐ plastic cartons or containers

☐ biscuit tins

☐ empty egg cartons

☐ plastic beakers

☐ plastic flower pots

Items for matching and sorting can also be used for sequencing tasks.

SECTION 13

APPENDIX I

Further Reading

Cooke J, *Early Sensory Skills,* Winslow, Bicester, 1996.

Cooke J & Harrisoon V, *How to Use Colour Cards in the Classroom,* Winslow, Bicester, 1998.

Cooke J & Williams D, *Working with Children's Language,* Winslow, Bicester, 1988.

Lear, R, *Play Helps (Toys and Activities for Handicapped Children),* 4th edn, Butterworth Heinemann, London, 1996.

Lynch C & Cooper J, *Early Communication Skills,* Winslow, Bicester, 1991.

Williams D, *Early Listening Skills,* Winslow, Bicester, 1995.

APPENDIX II

Useful Addresses

Toys, materials and equipment are available from the following companies by mail order:

United Kingdom

Early Learning Centre
South Marston
Swindon SN3 4TJ
(There are many high
street branches around
the country.)

ROMPA International
Goyt Side Road
Chesterfield
Derbyshire S40 2PH

TFH
76 Barracks Road
Sandy Lane Industrial Estate
Stourport-on-Severn
Worcestershire DY13 9QB

Taskmaster
Morris Road
Clarendon Park
Leicester LE2 6BR

Winslow Press Ltd
Telford Road
Bicester
Oxon OX6 0TS

United States of America

Applied Symbolix
800 North Wells Street,
Suite 200
Chicago,
IL 60610

Imaginart
307 Arizona Street
Bisbee
AZ 85603

**PCI Educational
Publishing Inc**
12029 Warfield
San Antonio
Texas 78216

S&S Worldwide
75 Mill Street
PO Box 513
Colchester
CT 06415

The Speech Bin
1965 Twenty-fifth Avenue
Vero Beach
Florida 32960

**Super Duper School
Company**
PO Box 24997
6000 Pelham Road
Greenville
SC 29615